Also by Louis Rukeyser

—————

How to Make Money in Wall Street

What's Ahead for the Economy:
The Challenge and the Chance

Louis Rukeyser's Business Almanac

LOUIS RUKEYSER'S BOOK OF LISTS

⊖ ⊖ ⊖

LOUIS RUKEYSER'S BOOK OF LISTS

The Best, the Worst,
and the Funniest from
the Worlds of Business,
Finance, and Politics

HENRY HOLT AND COMPANY   •   NEW YORK

Henry Holt and Company, Inc. / *Publishers since 1866*
115 West 18th Street / New York, New York 10011

Henry Holt® is a registered
trademark of Henry Holt and Company, Inc.

Published in Canada by Fitzhenry & Whiteside Ltd.,
195 Allstate Parkway, Markham, Ontario L3R 4T8.

Library of Congress Cataloging-in-Publication Data
Rukeyser, Louis.
Louis Rukeyser's book of lists: the best, the worst, and
the funniest from the worlds of business, finance, and
politics / Louis Rukeyser. — 1st ed.
p.   cm.
Includes bibliographical references.
ISBN 0-8050-5126-0 (hardcover: alk. paper)
1. Securities—Ratings—Miscellanea. 2. Investments—
Miscellanea. 3. Investments—Humor—Miscellanea. I. Title.
HG4527.R74   1997   97-23136
332.6—dc21   CIP

Henry Holt books are available for special promotions and
premiums. For details contact: Director, Special Markets.

First Edition 1997

Designed by Victoria Hartman

Printed in the United States of America
All first editions are printed on acid-free paper. ∞

1   3   5   7   9   10   8   6   4   2

An extension of this copyright appears on pages 259–260.

Contents

✑   ✑   ✑

Part 2 · It's Your Money

Part 4 · The Guys in Government

Part 5 · A World of Business

Part 6 · So Many Interesting People

Guest Contributors

⊖　　⊖　　⊖

FRANK CAPPIELLO is an expert on the national economy and a recognized authority on financial investments. A panelist on *Wall $treet Week With Louis Rukeyser,* he is also President of McCullough, Andrews & Cappiello, Inc., providing asset management to individual and institutional investors. The firm currently has $1.4 billion under management. He is also Chairman of Closed-End Fund Advisors, Inc. He is a panelist on *Wall $treet Week With Louis Rukeyser.*

HOWARD P. (PETE) COLHOUN is a founder and General Partner of Emerging Growth Partners of Baltimore, Maryland. Before the establishment of that company in 1982, he was President and Chairman of the Board of T. Rowe Price New Era Fund. Mr. Colhoun also serves on the Investment Committee of the State of Maryland Pension Fund, managing in excess of $24 billion. He is a panelist on *Wall $treet Week With Louis Rukeyser.*

ELIZABETH (BETH) DATER is a member of Warburg, Pincus Counsellors' Executive Operating Committee and is the Senior Investment Manager for a number of their funds, including Small-Cap Growth Equity, Small/Mid-Cap Growth Equity, Distribution Management, and Post-Venture Products. She earlier served as Director of Research for the company's investment management activities. Prior to joining Warburg, Pincus, Ms. Dater was Vice President of Research at Fiduciary Trust Company of New York. She is a panelist on *Wall $treet Week With Louis Rukeyser.*

MARY C. FARRELL is a managing director and member of the Investment Policy Committee for PaineWebber Incorporated. She specializes in strategy for small-capitalization issues. Ms. Farrell is regularly quoted in leading business publications and is a panelist on *Wall $treet Week With Louis Rukeyser.*

ELAINE GARZARELLI is a money manager and researcher at Garzarelli Investment Management. She was the number one quantitative strategist on Wall Street for eleven consecutive years, according to *Institutional Investor* magazine.

MICHAEL HOLLAND has had a long and successful career in the investment field. He started with J. P. Morgan in the late sixties and has served as CEO of Salomon Brothers Asset Management and First Boston Asset Management. He is currently the chairman of his own investment firm, Holland & Company, LLC, and is President and founder of Holland Balanced Fund. Mr. Holland is a panelist on *Wall $treet Week With Louis Rukeyser.*

JAMES R. JONES was the United States Ambassador to Mexico from August 1993 through May 1997. From 1989 to 1993 he was chairman and Chief Executive Officer of the American Stock Exchange. Mr. Jones also was a member of Congress from Oklahoma from 1973 to 1987, where he chaired the House Budget Committee from 1981 to 1985 and served as Deputy Majority Whip from 1975 to 1977.

KNIGHT A. KIPLINGER is editor-in-chief of *Kiplinger's Personal Finance Magazine* and coeditor of *The Kiplinger Washington Letter.* Mr. Kiplinger has moved the Kiplinger organization into several new fields, including videotapes, electronic information, and computer software. A native of Washington, D.C., he graduated from Cornell University and did graduate study in international affairs at Princeton University.

ARTHUR LEVITT has served as Chairman of the Securities and Exchange Commission since 1993. Earlier, he held a series of notable positions, including Chairman of the New York City Development Corporation

(1989 to 1993) and Chairman of the American Stock Exchange (1978 to 1989). Prior to accepting the AMEX chairmanship, Mr. Levitt worked for sixteen years on Wall Street.

JAMES C. MILLER III was an associate director of the Office of Management and Budget from January to October, 1981, where he set up President Reagan's program of regulatory relief. From October 1981 to October 1985 he was Chairman of the Federal Trade Commission, and from October 1985 to October 1988 he was Director of the Office of Management and Budget; he was a member of President Reagan's Cabinet and the National Security Council. He is currently a counselor to Citizens for a Sound Economy and is John M. Olin Distinguished Fellow at Citizens for a Sound Economy Foundation and at the Center for Study of Public Choice at George Mason University in Fairfax, Virginia.

BERNADETTE MURPHY has been a member of the rotating panel on *Wall $treet Week With Louis Rukeyser* for more than eighteen years. She is a managing director and senior money manager at Kimelman & Baird, LLC, and also serves as a consultant to professional money managers at banks, insurance companies, mutual funds, and pension funds. Ms. Murphy was the 1996 recipient of AIMR's Distinguished Service Award.

ROBERT NAGY is Associate Professor of Finance at the University of Wisconsin–Green Bay. He received his doctorate at Mississippi State University after enjoying stints as a securities analyst, bank portfolio manager, and pension fund manager. His publications include articles in the *Financial Analysts Journal,* the *Review of Financial Economics,* and the *Journal of Retail Banking Services.* Dr. Nagy is still looking for the miscreant who told him that 70-hour work weeks would become a thing of the past if he joined academia.

After service in World War II, WILLIAM PROXMIRE earned a degree in public administration from Harvard and then served as a teaching fellow at that institution from 1949 to 1950. He then took a position as a reporter on the Madison, Wisconsin, *Capital-Times* and was elected to the Wisconsin State Assembly in 1954 and to the United States Senate in 1957. He served as a U.S. senator until his retirement in 1988. His "Golden Fleece Awards" for governmental and business excesses received national attention and publicity.

DONALD H. RUMSFELD is currently Chairman of the Board of Gilead Sciences, Inc. Previously he served the United States in a number of major capacities, including U.S. Representative from Illinois, 1963–1969; member of the Cabinet of President Richard M. Nixon, 1969–1972; U.S. Ambassador to NATO, 1973–1974; White House Chief of Staff to President Gerald R. Ford, 1974–1975; and Secretary of Defense, the youngest in history, 1975–1977. From 1977 to 1996 he served successively as Chairman and CEO of G. D. Searle & Co. and at General Instrument Company, and as Chairman of the RAND Corporation. In 1977, he received the Presidential Medal of Freedom, the nation's highest civilian award.

CHARLES R. SCHWAB is founder, Chairman of the Board, and Chief Executive Officer of The Charles Schwab Corporation, one of the nation's largest brokerage firms, currently serving more than four million active investors whose accounts total more than $250 billion. Mr. Schwab is also a member of the board of trustees of Stanford University, serves as the treasurer and a member of the board of the National Park Foundation, and is Chairman of the Parent's Educational Resource Center, a nonprofit agency providing support and guidance for parents of children with learning differences.

WILLIAM E. SIMON is a former Secretary of the Treasury. A past president of the United States Olympic Committee, he is Chairman of William E. Simon & Sons and President of the John M. Olin Foundation.

MACEO K. SLOAN is Chairman, President, and CEO of both Sloan Financial Group, Inc., and NCM Capital Management Group, Inc., and also serves as Chairman of New Africa Advisers, Inc. Mr. Sloan is an attorney active in civic and professional affairs, including being the founder of the National Investment Managers Association, and serving on the Board of Directors and as a Trustee of a number of organizations, including the College Retirement Equities Fund (CREF). He is a panelist on *Wall $treet Week With Louis Rukeyser.*

ROBERT H. STOVALL has been a securities and market analyst for more than forty years. A professor of finance at New York University's Stern Graduate School of Business, he was also a partner or voting stockholder of E. F. Hutton & Company, John Nuveen, and Dean Witter Reynolds from 1961 through late 1985. Since September 1985, he has been President and Chief Investment Officer of Stovall/Twenty-First Advisers, Inc., a money management firm. He is a panelist on *Wall $treet Week With Louis Rukeyser.*

MURRAY WEIDENBAUM has been an economist in three worlds: business, government, and academia. He holds the Mallinckrodt Distinguished University Professorship at Washington University in St. Louis, where he also serves as Chairman of the University's Center for the Study of American Business. In 1981 and 1982, Dr. Weidenbaum was President Reagan's first Chairman of the Council of Economic Advisers; from 1983 to 1989, he served as a member of the President's Economic Advisory Board. Earlier, he was the Assistant Secretary of the Treasury for Economic Policy in the Nixon Administration. He also served as the Corporate Economist at the Boeing Company.

JULIUS WESTHEIMER is a Special Managing Director of Ferris, Baker Watts, Inc., a member of the New York Stock Exchange. He is also a panelist on *Wall $treet Week With Louis Rukeyser,* stock-market columnist for *The Baltimore Sun,* and financial broadcaster for WBAL radio and television. Despite all this, he confesses that he has trouble balancing his checkbook.

An Introductory Note from Lou

⊖　⊖　⊖

It all started with Moses, trundling down Mount Sinai with a list of the Lord's top ten Commandments. (Why not nine? Why not eleven? Somebody up there clearly knew what He was doing.) Moses' cargo became a paradigm for several millennia's worth of subsequent lists: it was brilliant, it was cogent, it was concise, and, in the clutch, it was widely ignored.

Still, the human compulsion to make lists has been inextinguishable. Many of us could not get through a typically overcrowded day without first preparing a list of what we have to accomplish. Sometimes, by nightfall, we even get to cross off all the items, an achievement that should, in a more properly ordered world, entitle us to a half-holiday.

Shoppers traditionally have been told to make lists before leaving home, and on a full stomach. Such lists may vary in complexity; a probably apocryphal story tells of finding a shopping list prepared by the late newspaper tycoon William Randolph Hearst, including only two requested purchases: "One croup kettle. Two hippopotami."

So lists can be useful, instructive—and, perhaps most of all, fun. They help us learn from others and order our own minds, from the teenage girl's "Five Boys in My Class I Would Never Go Out With, No Matter What" to the Lord High Executioner, in Gilbert and Sullivan's *The Mikado,* proclaiming with delicious malice: "As some day it may happen that a victim must be found, / I've got a little list, I've got a little list / Of society offenders who might well be underground, / And who never would be missed, who never would be missed."

On a less sinister note, the Scottish poet Robert Burns wrote, a century earlier: "Gif ye want ae friend that's true, / I'm on your list." Definitely a more genial fellow, Robbie was; and you'll find his spirit as well as that of William S. Gilbert in the pages of this book.

In fact, one of the happy surprises in putting this book together was discovering the pervasive attraction of list-making for so many extraordinarily prominent people. Among the friends who responded with amazing alacrity to my invitation to participate was the former Secretary of the Treasury, William E. Simon, who is represented in these pages with no fewer than nine characteristically opinionated and incisive lists. Their pungency makes clear that while Bill was making historic waves in the worlds of government and investment, he was also making more than a few memorable mental lists. Similarly, Donald H. Rumsfeld, who became America's youngest Secretary of Defense before launching an impressive business career, is on board with four revealing and good-humored lists; Don's erudition is so ecumenical that he manages to quote sources ranging from General Joe Stillwell ("The higher a monkey climbs, the more you see of his behind") to his own daughter, Marcy, at age seven ("It takes everyone to make a happy day"). I'm with Marcy.

On the other side of the political fence, retired Democratic Senator William Proxmire lets us in on his all-time list of favorite "Golden Fleece" awards, which he presented monthly for nearly 14 years to what he considered outstanding examples of frivolous government spending. ($45 million for a study on how to cut toenails? Only in America.) Bill demonstrates again how his exceptional career belatedly validated the dictum of Kansas' Governor Alf Landon, the luckless presidential candidate of 1936, who plaintively declared: "I believe a man can be a liberal without being a spendthrift."

Not surprisingly, the habitually haywire antics along the Potomac inspired other list-makers, too. Murray Weidenbaum, the astute economist who is our greatest living expert on the excesses of well-meaning government regulators, is absolutely unhedged about what he calls the "Ten Silliest Federal Regulations." (A Braille keypad for blind drivers? Hmmm. It might be time for some of those bureaucrats to get out of the office more.) On a more upbeat note, former budget director James C. Miller III eschews polemics and reminds us, in two possibly startling lists, that we have actually managed sometimes to *reduce* the national debt—and that, believe it or not, the federal government has run a *surplus* in virtually as many years as it has run a deficit. The numbers Jim assembles may well surprise you, given the conventional assumptions about perennial deficits—not to mention the legendary shortness of the American memory span (which I once calculated at 19.4 seconds)—but I kid you not.

Many of our guest contributors are equally provocative when it comes to your own money. Arthur Levitt, who has been the chief cop on the financial integrity beat as Chairman of the Securities and Exchange Commission since 1993, gives us "Top Ten Questions to Ask Your Broker." (If the brokers balk, tell them Art sent you.) Knight Kiplinger distills the wisdom of three generations of eminent personal-finance advisers into "Eight Keys to Financial Security." And we get wonderfully useful information, advice, and market lore from some of the illustrious stars who are known both for their own impressive achievements and for their appearances as my guests and panelists on television: Frank Cappiello, Pete Colhoun, Beth Dater, Mary Farrell, Elaine Garzarelli, Mike Holland, Jim Jones, Bernadette Murphy, Charles Schwab, Maceo Sloan, Bob Stovall, and Julius Westheimer. My thanks to them all for letting us in on their favorite lists.

As you'll quickly see, while the making of lists is almost by definition a didactic, self-confident exercise (how do you think those boys would have felt if they had known they were on the teenage girl's never-to-be-dated list?), it can also be accompanied by an engaging amount of self-deprecating humility. Julius Westheimer, at 80, might understandably feel that it was time for him to start claiming Moses-like infallibility—plenty of his less-knowledgeable juniors do it all the time—but instead Westy decided to confess "Julius Westheimer's Ten Biggest Mistakes in the Market." (When a youthful octogenarian displays that kind of charming and unusual candor, you know he has a bright career ahead of him.) By our lists you shall know us.

And while I'm handing out words of appreciation, let me thank what is at least the second-greatest team in Green Bay, Wisconsin: Professor Emeritus Martin Greenberg, whose creativeness and enthusiasm inspired this book, and the research colleagues who helped implement it so carefully and responsibly, Professor Robert Nagy and Professor William Lepley. All are associated with the University of Wisconsin–Green Bay, and they should make the Packers proud. Warm thanks go, too, to Larry Segriff, John Helfers, and Marlys Brunsting for their unfailing diligence in preparing the manuscript, and to my ever-perspicacious editor at Henry Holt, Cynthia Vartan. In the immortal words of Casey Stengel, I couldn't have done it without the players.

One final note as you peruse these pages, and learn such presumably invaluable facts as "The Best Countries in the World to Open a Liquor Store" (based on the percent of consumption spending on alcohol, the relatively sober U.S. ranks way down the list): there is much to argue about here, as well as much to learn. Even the lists that are purely statistical—if that's not an oxymoron—may scratch your brainpan and engender some lively discussion. Take what *Fortune* calls its list of the "Most Generous People in the United States." These folks are undeniably impressive contributors to the causes of their choice, but when a billionaire donates, say, $30 million, does that make him more generous than an ordinary family that stretches to give $3,000? The former is certainly a more alluring target for the nation's fund-raisers, but is his philanthropic impulse necessarily greater?

And some lists may simply be based on wishful thinking. While those surveyed for "Tips on Tipping" offered some useful guidance, for example, I wonder how many skycaps could honestly tell you that they typically get $4 for checking a single bag? And can room-service waiters really count on 20% tips? Such entries, while they may spur some travelers to be a bit more forthcoming, remind me of the story, older than any of us, of the Pullman porter early in this century who was asked by a novice traveler what was the average tip after an overnight stay on the train. "Five dollars, sir," said the porter. The traveler was somewhat taken aback, but dutifully forked over a fiver.

"Thank you so much, sir!" exclaimed the porter. "I've been working on this railroad for 35 years, and you're the first person who has come up to the average."

So, like the Pullman porter, feel free to start making your own little lists. And I hope, at the top, will be: enjoy and have fun with this book.

LOUIS RUKEYSER'S BOOK OF LISTS

PART

• 1 •

Those Mad, Mad Markets

Arthur Levitt's Top Ten Questions
to Ask Your Broker

1. Has any action ever been brought against you, by either a client or a regulator?

2. When you recommend a product to me, will you tell me if you stand to gain a bonus, higher commission, or a prize if I agree to buy it?

3. What is the risk involved in this investment, and how does that suit my investing profile?

4. How liquid is this investment (how easily can I sell it)?

5. What is your personal investment philosophy?

6. Could you describe your typical client (include age, economic status, and risk aversion at least)?

7. Could you give me the name of a long-term client I could call for a reference?

8. How do you get paid (commissions, amount of assets under management, or flat fee)?

9. Will you alert me if you notice a trend in my financial activities that does not match my investment goals?

10. Are you willing to put all of the above statements, and other verbal guarantees, in writing?

The Best-Performing Stocks
on the New York Stock Exchange in 1996

Stock	Return (%)
Centennial Technologies	451
Converse	312
Flores & Rucks	267
Miller Industries	264
RMI Titanium	252
Fairfield Communities	247
Western Digital	218
United Meridian	191
Royal Appliance Manufacturing	175
CompUSA	167
Genesco	164
Shaw Group	163
NGC	162

The Worst-Performing Stocks
on the New York Stock Exchange in 1996

Stock	Return (%)
FoxMeyer Health	−93
EA Industries	−92
Amre	−89
Mid-American Waste Systems	−88
Marvel Entertainment Group	−87
Buenos Aires Embotelladora	−82
Alliance Entertainment	−80
GRC International	−78
Kerr Group	−76
Penn Traffic	−76

Pete Colhoun's Nine Favorite Investment Sayings

1. Don't confuse wisdom with a bull market.

2. There are three sides to every story—yours, mine, and the facts.

3. Change is the investor's only certainty.

4. The biggest decisions in life are emotionally made and then intellectually justified, not vice versa.

5. It's what you learn after you know it all that counts.

6. If you don't know where you are going, you will end up somewhere else.

7. One has to be able to handle defeat and come back from it. To be successful, you have to have a bit of the phoenix in you.

8. Remember, the very best baseball batters hit the ball safely only about one third of the time. Two thirds of the time they fail.

9. I would rather be vaguely right than precisely wrong.

The Best-Performing NASDAQ Stocks of 1996

Stock	Return (%)
TSR	967
VIASOFT	696
Zitel	640
ISG International Software Group	517
Federal Agricultural Mortgage	515
Finish Line	463
PMR	436
Williams Energy	435
Maxwell Technologies	433
Medicis Pharmaceutical	376
Ultrak	374
Encad	371
ASV	337
SBS Technology	335
Zoltek	334
Pacific Sunwear	329

The Worst-Performing NASDAQ Stocks of 1996

Stock	Return (%)
Best Products	−99.7
NeoStar Retail Group	−98.0
Biosys	−98.0
MobileMedia	−98.0
Com/Tech	−98.0
TPI Enterprises	−97.0
SC&T International	−97.0
China Resources	−96.0
Videolan	−95.0
Embryo Development	−95.0
International Cutlery	−94.0
Italian Oven	−94.0
Network Six	−94.0
Health Management	−93.0
Chantal	−93.0
Reddi Brake	−92.0
Computron Software	−92.0

Mary Farrell's List of the Top Ten Euphemisms When an Investment Is Wrong

1. The company's expenses were unexpectedly high. *(I overestimated margins.)*

2. Sales were less than expected. *(I didn't notice all those competitors who were fighting for market share.)*

3. Unseasonably cold weather hurt sales in the first quarter. *(Of course, it's always cold January through March, but I don't want to admit I was wrong.)*

4. Earnings were disappointing. *(Not for the company, which was right on plan, but I was hoping for a miracle to bail out this recommendation.)*

5. We had a major earnings shortfall. *(I don't have a clue what is going on with this company.)*

6. I'm fine-tuning my estimate. *(What's a 50-percent cut among friends?)*

7. Although our long-term recommendation remains intact, there are a few short-term problems. *(Thank God, in the long run we are all dead and I won't have to answer for this fiasco.)*

8. Management is unavailable for comment. *(At least I've bought a little time to think up a creative explanation for this disaster.)*

9. This correction is a good buying opportunity. *(Stock's in free fall.)*

10. I'm downgrading to a neutral. *(SELL SELL SELL.)*

The Best-Performing AMEX Stocks of 1996

Stock	1996 Return
Saba Petroleum	562.2
UTI Energy	528.9
TransMontaign	260.0
National Beverage	234.8
Bema Gold	196.9
Ion Laser Technology	193.3
Keane, Inc.	187.0
Norex Industries	180.0
Bay Meadows Operating	179.5
Ballantyne of Omaha	171.1

The Worst-Performing AMEX Stocks of 1996

Stock	1996 Return
Datametrics	−86.5
Interline Resources	−84.3
Unilab Corp.	−83.7
PC Quote	−83.5
Kleer Vu Industries	−82.1
Editek	−78.3
Omni Multimedia Group	−71.3
Leather Factory	−66.7
Stevens International "A"	−65.7
Electrochemical Industries	−64.3

Mike Holland's Six Most Useful
Books on Investing

1. *Security Analysis,* by Benjamin Graham, David Dodd, and Sidney Cottle

2. *Extraordinary Popular Delusions and the Madness of Crowds,* by Charles Mackay

3. *Stocks for the Long Run,* by Jeremy Siegel

4. *Reminiscences of a Stock Market Speculator,* by Edwin Le Fevre

5. *Battle for Investment Survival,* by Gerald M. Loeb

6. The Bible

❖ THEN *and* NOW ❖

Chairman of General Motors' Annual Salary

• • •

1946 actual salary: $196,620
1946 salary, adjusted for inflation: $1.7 million

1995 actual salary: $3.3 million

Bob Stovall's The Stock Market
and the United States Political Cycle

Many technical analysts believe that the performance of the
stock market is closely linked to stages in the presidential political cycle. They argue that the governors of the Federal Reserve
System tend to follow easy money policies in the last two years of
a president's term as a means of stimulating economic growth.
These efforts often result in booming equity markets and en-
hanced political prospects for the party occupying the White
House. This theory has been borne out in eight of the last nine
political cycles. Did I mention that Fed governors are appointed
by the president?

President	Years of First Half Term	Period's Average Dow Return (%)	Years of Second Half Term	Period's Average Dow Return (%)
Kennedy-Johnson	1961–62	4.0	1963–64	15.80
Johnson	1965–66	−4.0	1967–68	9.70
Nixon	1969–70	−5.2	1971–72	10.30
Nixon	1973–74	−22.1	1975–76	28.10
Carter	1977–78	−10.2	1979–80	9.60
Reagan	1981–82	5.2	1983–84	8.30
Reagan	1985–86	25.1	1987–88	7.10
Bush	1989–90	11.3	1991–92	12.30
Clinton	1993–94	7.9	1995–96	29.75

S&P 500 Firms with Five Consecutive Years of Earnings Increases of 15 Percent or More, 1992–1996

Company	5-Year Earnings-per-Share Growth Rate (%)
Southwest Airlines	40
Green Tree Financial	35
Medtronic, Inc.	25
Home Depot, Inc.	23
Monsanto Co.	23
Dover Corp.	22
MBNA Corp.	22
Illinois Tool Works	19
Johnson Controls	17
Albertson's, Inc.	16
Coca-Cola Co.	16
Pep Boys—Manny, Moe, & Jack	16
Fifth Third Bancorp	15
Norwest Corp.	15
Service Corp. International	15

❖ THEN *and* NOW ❖

Months an Average Worker Had
to Work to Pay for a New Car

• • •

1947: 4.8

1997: 5.3

Dividend Yields of S&P 500 Firms with Ten Years of Continuously Increasing Dividends, 1986–1996, That Currently Yield at Least 3 Percent

Firm	*Dividend Yield (%)*
Consolidated Edison	7.2
Central & South West Corp.	6.7
Union Electric	6.7
Northern States Power	5.9
Peoples Energy	5.4
Philip Morris Cos.	5.1
UST Inc.	4.9
Bell Atlantic Corp.	4.8
H & R Block	4.7
Duke Power	4.4
Potlatch Corp.	4.2
Lincoln National Corp.	3.9
Ameritech Corp.	3.7
J. P. Morgan	3.7
Exxon Corp.	3.6
Marsh & McLennan	3.6
ALLTEL Corp.	3.5
SBC Communications	3.5
First Union Corp.	3.4
H. J. Heinz	3.4
KeyCorp	3.4
Luby's Cafeterias	3.4
Supervalu Inc.	3.4
Banc One Corp.	3.3
National Service Industries	3.2
Wachovia Corp.	3.2
International Flavors & Fragrances, Inc.	3.1

Firm	Dividend Yield (%)
SAFECO Corp.	3.1
The St. Paul Companies, Inc.	3.1
U.S. Bancorp	3.1
Bristol-Myers Squibb	3.0
Comerica Inc.	3.0
USLIFE Corp.	3.0

❖ THEN *and* NOW ❖

Auto Worker's Annual Salary

• • •

1947 average salary: $2,770
1947 average salary, adjusted for inflation: $20,410

1996 average salary: $39,540

S&P 500 Stocks with Earnings Growth
of 15 Percent or More, 1991–1996

Company	5-Year Earnings-per-Share Growth (%)
Applied Materials	89
EMC Corp.	79
Green Tree Financial	35
Andrew Corp.	35
Columbia/HCA Healthcare Corp.	27
Medtronic, Inc.	25
Avery Dennison Corp.	24
MGIC Investment	24
Home Depot	23
MBNA	22
Gillette Co.	17
Albertson's Inc.	16
Norwest Corp.	15

S&P 500 Firms with Dividend Growth of 20 Percent or More, 1991–1996

Company	Dividend Growth Rate (%)
Goodyear Tire & Rubber Co.	41.03
Mattel, Inc.	37.29
Home Depot, Inc.	33.67
Green Tree Financial	30.33
Hewlett-Packard	29.72
Archer Daniels Midland	29.58
Sysco Corp.	28.92
Travelers Group	27.88
Medtronic, Inc.	25.47
Federal National Mortgage	24.48
Circuit City Stores	23.58
Wal-Mart Stores	22.08
Barrick Gold	21.04
Walt Disney Co.	20.90
Nucor Corp.	20.67
Hasbro Inc.	20.18

The 25 Quarters of *Highest* Dividend Yield, 1935–1997*

Rank	Year—Quarter	Dividend Yield (%)
1	1938—1	9.20
2	1942—1	8.64
3	1941—4	8.19
4	1942—2	7.95
5	1937—4	7.62
6	1951—2	7.45
7	1950—4	7.20
8	1949—2	7.18
9	1951—1	7.11
10	1942—3	7.06
11	1941—2	7.00
12	1941—3	6.91
13	1950—3	6.86
14	1941—1	6.84
15	1949—4	6.79
16	1950—2	6.77
17	1950—1	6.76
18	1949—3	6.67
19	1940—2	6.56
20	1951—3	6.55
21	1949—1	6.50
22	1938—2	6.37
23	1940—4	6.34
24	1940—3	6.32
25	1982—2	6.21

* Through the first quarter of 1997.

The 25 Quarters of *Lowest* Dividend Yield, 1935–1997*

Rank	Year—Quarter	Dividend Yield (%)
1	1997—1	1.88
2	1996—4	2.01
3	1996—3	2.13
4	1996—2	2.13
5	1996—1	2.18
6	1995—4	2.24
7	1995—3	2.32
8	1995—2	2.45
9	1995—1	2.63
10	1972—4	2.67
11	1987—3	2.69
12	1993—4	2.70
13	1993—3	2.73
14	1993—1	2.76
15	1993—2	2.78
16	1972—3	2.79
17	1994—3	2.79
18	1987—2	2.80
19	1961—4	2.82
20	1973—1	2.84
21	1992—4	2.84
22	1994—1	2.85
23	1987—1	2.86
24	1972—1	2.86
25	1972—2	2.87

* Through the first quarter of 1997.

The 25 Quarters of *Highest*
P/E (Price/Earnings) Ratio, 1935–1997*

Rank	Year—Quarter	P/E Ratio
1	1991—4	26.10
2	1992—1	24.90
3	1992—2	23.90
4	1993—2	23.30
5	1992—3	23.20
6	1993—1	22.80
7	1992—4	22.80
8	1993—3	22.50
9	1961—4	22.43
10	1946—2	21.94
11	1961—3	21.88
12	1991—3	21.80
13	1938—3	21.47
14	1961—2	21.33
15	1993—4	21.30
16	1987—2	21.06
17	1961—1	21.06
18	1996—4	21.00
19	1962—1	20.64
20	1997—1	20.40
21	1987—3	20.29
22	1938—2	20.28
23	1994—1	19.60
24	1987—1	19.32
25	1971—1	19.22

* Through the first quarter of 1997.

The 25 Quarters of *Lowest*
P/E (Price/Earnings) Ratio, 1935–1997*

Rank	Year—Quarter	P/E Ratio
1	1949—2	5.90
2	1949—1	6.33
3	1949—3	6.52
4	1948—4	6.64
5	1980—1	6.68
6	1950—2	6.96
7	1974—3	6.97
8	1950—3	7.15
9	1950—4	7.19
10	1949—4	7.22
11	1979—4	7.26
12	1950—1	7.30
13	1979—2	7.36
14	1979—3	7.47
15	1948—3	7.48
16	1951—1	7.56
17	1982—1	7.56
18	1979—1	7.64
19	1980—2	7.65
20	1942—1	7.70
21	1974—4	7.71
22	1981—3	7.71
23	1951—2	7.71
24	1982—2	7.74
25	1978—4	7.79

* Through the first quarter of 1997.

Beth Dater's Post–Venture Capital Index

For approximately the past thirty-five years American industry has consistently reinvented itself and maintained a worldwide technological lead through the support and backing of its vibrant venture capital community. Venture capital sponsorship may be broadly defined to include the funding of company start-ups, management buyouts, and the investment of substantial amounts of equity in financial restructurings.

Venture-backed companies typically develop innovative technologies, products, and services that create dynamic growth opportunities across a broad range of industries. Through the participation of venture capital partners, venture-financed companies have greater access to the capital necessary for research and development as well as other critical resources such as management, accounting and legal support, and other professional contacts. Managers of venture-backed entities typically hold a substantial equity stake in their companies, a factor that provides them with a significant incentive to succeed.

Because of the diligence with which both the venture capitalist and the entrepreneur have nurtured their investment, companies in their "post-venture" lives in the public equity markets offer investors above-average growth opportunities and long-term returns. Consider the names dominating the U.S. corporate landscape today that have received venture capital backing over the past thirty years. They include Digital Equipment, Federal Express, Intel, Mattel, Microsoft, Starbucks Corp., and United Healthcare, to name a few.

In 1966, my firm developed a Post–Venture Capital Index (PVCI) in association with Venture Economics, the publishers of *The Venture Capital Journal.* The PVCI is a market-valued index that measures the performance of companies that received financing from a U.S. venture capital or buyout limited partnership prior to or during public trading status, without dividends. Companies remain in the index for ten years from the first date of inclusion or until price data are no longer available, as in the case of a merger or acquisition. Special thanks to Jess Reyes of Venture Economics for assistance with these lists.

Beth Dater's List of Top Performers, Based on Total Returns of Venture-Backed Companies Going Public

1966–1975

Name	Total Return (millions of dollars)
Applied Materials, Inc.	7,060.0
Medtronic, Inc.	4,763.6
Intel Corp.	4,014.6
Sealed Air Corp.	1,317.4
Western Digital Corp.	1,267.5
Southwest Airlines Co.	844.8
Comcast Corp.	877.0
ALZA Corp.	766.7
MCI Communications Corp.	725.0
Arrow Electronics	614.9

1976–1985

Name	Total Return (millions of dollars)
Celutel, Inc.	13,875.0
Novell, Inc.	7,532.1
Paychex, Inc.	5,266.6
Daig Corporation	4,452.1
Compaq Computer	4,398.5
Home Depot, Inc.	4,240.5
Amgen, Inc. (FKA: Applied Mole)	4,030.4
IOMEGA	3,772.5
3COM	3,658.3
Symbol Technologies	3,088.0

1986–1996

Name	Total Return (millions of dollars)
International Microcomputer	18,750.0
Microsoft	16,873.9
Cisco Systems	11,190.1
Solectron	7,433.1
Parametric Technology	5,750.0
Dell Computer	4,454.8
Maxim Integrated Products	3,645.5
Adaptec	3,403.9
Electronic Arts	3,112.5
Cascade Communications	2,910.0

1966–1996

Name	Total Return (millions of dollars)
International Microcomputer	18,750.0
Microsoft	16,873.9
Celutel, Inc.	13,875.0
Cisco Systems	11,190.1
Novell, Inc.	7,532.1
Solectron	7,433.3
Applied Materials, Inc.	7,060.0
Parametric Technology	5,750.0
Paychex, Inc.	5,266.6

The Top Private Placement Agents in 1996

Manager	Private Placement Proceeds (billions of dollars)
1. Merrill Lynch	15.2
2. J. P. Morgan	13.7
3. Credit Suisse First Boston	11.6
4. Morgan Stanley	11.1
5. Goldman, Sachs	9.1
6. Donaldson, Lufkin & Jenrette	8.5
7. Salomon Brothers	8.2
8. Lehman Brothers	7.6
9. Bear, Stearns	6.7
10. BankAmerica	6.4
11. Chase Manhattan Corp.	6.3
12. Citicorp	4.6
13. Smith Barney, Inc.	3.5
14. Bankers Trust	2.8
15. Bank of Tokyo–Mitsubishi	2.5
16. NationsBank	2.1
17. CIBC Wood Gundy Securities	2.0
18. UBS	1.7
19. Deutsche Morgan Grenfell	1.6
20. ING Barings	1.5
21. Schroder Group	1.4
22. Dillon, Read	1.3
23. Nesbitt Burns Securities	1.2
24. SBC Warburg	1.2
25. NatWest Markets	1.2

The Top Ten Underwriters, Ranked by Disclosed Fees in 1996

Firm	Gross Spread (millions of dollars)
Merrill Lynch	1,335
Goldman, Sachs	1,205
Morgan Stanley	882
Donaldson, Lufkin & Jenrette	647
Smith Barney	564
Salomon Brothers	492
Lehman Brothers	488
Credit Suisse First Boston	422
Alex. Brown & Sons	322
J. P. Morgan	250

❖ THEN *and* NOW ❖

Yearly Tuition at Harvard

• • •

1947 tuition: $525
1947 tuition, adjusted for inflation: $3,870

1997 tuition: $19,770

The Top Ten Underwriters of
Domestic Debt and Equity in 1996

Firm	Proceeds (billions of dollars)
Merrill Lynch	155.9
Lehman Brothers	100.7
Goldman, Sachs	98.5
Salomon Brothers	96.2
Morgan Stanley	83.7
J. P. Morgan	68.7
Credit Suisse First Boston	60.0
Bear, Stearns	41.7
Donaldson, Lufkin & Jenrette	34.5
Smith Barney	29.9

The Top Ten Equity Underwriters in 1996

Firm	*Proceeds* *(billions of dollars)*
Goldman, Sachs	16.6
Merrill Lynch	14.2
Morgan Stanley	12.6
Donaldson, Lufkin, & Jenrette	8.0
Smith Barney	7.9
Salomon Brothers	5.8
Credit Suisse First Boston	5.6
Alex. Brown & Sons	5.5
Lehman Brothers	4.6
Montgomery Securities	4.3

Pete Colhoun's Ten Most Important Things to Do to Be a Successful Investor

1. Keep it simple. Say no to complicated financial products. Don't own too many items in a portfolio. Let others do the bookkeeping.

2. Own stocks for appreciation. The largest percentage of your long-term holdings should be stocks or stock mutual funds, not bonds. The younger one is, or the longer away the need for the asset is, the higher the percent of stocks versus bonds.

3. Realize that asset allocation is much more important than item picking. Ninety percent or more of what determines the outcome or investment performance of *any* portfolio is asset allocation—the relative proportions of assets in seven or eight categories (large capitalization stocks, small capitalization stocks, international stocks, cash or money market funds, domestic bonds, real estate, and tangible assets like diamonds, paintings, etc.). Item picking—Stock X versus Stock Y—contributes a much, much smaller portion.

4. Stay diversified. Own all the major asset classes and don't put all your eggs in one basket.

5. Minimize taxes. Maximize assets in tax-deferred plans such as IRAs and IRA rollovers, and 403(b), 401(k), and pension and profit-sharing plans. Where possible, choose long-term capital gains opportunities versus ordinary income-taxed situations, for two reasons: capital gains rates are less than ordinary income tax rates, and income taxes are due annually, whereas capital gains taxes are postponed until a sale is made—maybe years later.

6. Have patience. The power of compound appreciation is tremendous. An investment growing at 15 percent a year doubles in less than five years. Let your money multiply and don't make multiple short-term trades.

7. Be contrarian. Buy "straw hats in January," when no one else wants them and prices are lower.

8. Have a plan. Know what you are trying to accomplish and stick with it.

9. Know yourself. Most people are their own worst investment enemy. Don't take chances if you can't sleep comfortably with a risk.

10. Know what you are doing. Get quarterly data and focus particularly on annual or multiyear performance.

The Ten Busiest Trading Days
on the New York Stock Exchange, 1980–1997*

Date	Number of Shares Traded
January 23, 1997	683,800,820
July 16, 1996	680,308,000
June 20, 1997	652,725,670
December 20, 1996	650,065,430
December 15, 1996	636,790,000
October 20, 1987	608,120,000
October 19, 1987	604,330,000
June 25, 1997	603,019,530
January 24, 1997	593,000,000
February 13, 1997	584,368,420

*Through June 30, 1997.

❖ **THEN** *and* NOW ❖

Yearly Tuition at the University of Iowa

• • •

1947 costs: $130
1947 costs, adjusted for inflation: $960

1997 costs: $2,470

Frank Cappiello's List
of U.S. Bear and Bull Markets

Seven Longest Bear Markets Since 1966

Start	End	Approximate Number of Months
January 1973	December 1974	23
September 1978	April 1980	19
December 1968	May 1970	17
September 1976	February 1978	17
April 1981	August 1982	16
February 1966	October 1966	8
November 1983	July 1984	8

Seven Longest Bull Markets Since 1966

Start	End	Approximate Number of Months
October 1990	*	*
July 1984	August 1987	37
October 1987	July 1990	33
October 1966	December 1968	26
December 1974	September 1976	21
August 1982	November 1983	15
November 1971	January 1973	14

*The bull market continues as of July 1, 1997.

Thirteen Categories of
Top-Performing Mutual Funds

The following 13 lists represent the top mutual funds in their category, ranked according to three-year returns. In ranking these funds, *Louis Rukeyser's Mutual Funds* newsletter considered funds with managers in place for at least three years; the only exceptions are managers with at least three years' experience in a similar capacity. They did not rank funds with front- or back-end loads greater than 3 percent or funds that are closed to new investors, have less than $50 million in assets, have minimums of $100,000 or more, have trust restrictions, or are single-state muni-bond funds. All data are as of May 31, 1997.

The Top-Performing Mutual Funds, Category 1: Aggressive Growth

Fund	1-Year Total Return (%)	3-Year Annual Return (%)	5-Year Annual Return (%)
Rydex OTC	41.4	36.9	N/A
Rydex Nova	38.7	32.4	N/A
Robertson Stephens Value+Growth	23.9	29.3	25.1
Westwood Equity	24.8	25.8	20.1
Janus Twenty	25.3	24.8	16.1
Warburg Pincus Capital Appreciation	22.7	23.8	18.2
Average for all funds in sector	7.2	17.0	14.3

The Top-Performing Mutual Funds, Category 2: Small-Company Growth

Fund	1-Year Total Return (%)	3-Year Annual Return (%)	5-Year Annual Return (%)
Dreyfus Small Company Value	24.4	25.9	N/A
PBHG Emerging Growth	−17.8	25.8	N/A
Baron Asset	6.3	25.1	21.9
Kaufmann	1.5	23.7	21.8
Neuberger & Berman Genesis Fund	23.5	23.5	17.2
Average for all funds in sector	3.9	18.3	16.4

The Top-Performing Mutual Funds, Category 3: Long-Term Growth

Fund	1-Year Total Return (%)	3-Year Annual Return (%)	5-Year Annual Return (%)
White Oak Growth Stock	30.6	34.2	N/A
Legg Mason Value Trust	45.5	31.9	22.8
Stein Roe Young Investor	17.9	29.3	N/A
Vanguard Index Growth	33.2	28.8	N/A
Torray Fund	30.5	28.6	20.3
Dreyfus Appreciation	31.7	28.6	17.1
Dreyfus Large Company Value	27.7	27.5	N/A
Vanguard U.S. Growth	28.6	27.2	17.0
Vanguard/Primecap	26.5	27.0	22.4
Selected American Shares	37.4	25.8	18.1
Average for all funds in sector	17.7	19.9	15.3

The Top-Performing Mutual Funds, Category 4: Total Return Growth and Income

Fund	1-Year Total Return (%)	3-Year Annual Return (%)	5-Year Annual Return (%)
Vanguard Index 500 Portfolio	29.3	25.8	18.2
BT Investment Equity 500 Index	29.3	25.7	N/A
Seven Seas S&P 500 Index	29.1	25.6	N/A
T. Rowe Price Equity Index	29.1	25.6	18.0
Fidelity Spartan Market Index	28.9	25.5	18.0
Galaxy II Large Company Index	29.0	25.5	17.9
Dreyfus S&P 500 Index	28.8	25.2	17.8
American Century Income & Growth	27.6	25.1	18.6
Vanguard Growth & Income	27.3	24.8	18.3
Westcore Blue Chip	24.3	24.5	17.3
Average for all funds in sector	22.8	21.0	15.9

The Top-Performing Mutual Funds, Category 5: Blended Growth and Income

Fund	1-Year Total Return (%)	3-Year Annual Return (%)	5-Year Annual Return (%)
Montgomery Asset Allocation	11.1	22.9	N/A
Invesco Balanced	15.2	21.2	N/A
Vanguard Asset Allocation	22.2	20.5	15.6
Vanguard/Wellington	21.9	19.2	14.9
Founders Balanced	20.0	18.5	N/A
Preferred Asset Allocation	18.9	18.5	N/A
Average for all funds in sector	15.6	15.3	12.0

The Top-Performing Mutual Funds, Category 6: Specialty Industry Sector

Fund	1-Year Total Return (%)	3-Year Annual Return (%)	5-Year Annual Return (%)
Vanguard Special Health	23.7	36.7	20.6
T. Rowe Price Science & Technology	2.3	30.3	25.6
Invesco Strategic Technology	10.6	27.0	22.7
Invesco Strategic Health	4.8	26.1	12.5
Invesco Strategic Financial	37.4	25.9	21.9
Average for all funds in sector	N/A	N/A	N/A

The Top-Performing Mutual Funds,
Category 7: Specialty Regional International

Fund	1-Year Total Return (%)	3-Year Annual Return (%)	5-Year Annual Return (%)
Fidelity Europe	22.0	19.4	14.1
T. Rowe Price European Stock	20.1	18.9	13.4
Vanguard International Index European	25.4	18.8	13.7
Invesco European	21.2	16.8	11.2
Fidelity Europe Capital Appreciation	26.5	15.4	N/A
Average for all funds in sector	N/A	N/A	N/A

The Top-Performing Mutual Funds,
Category 8: Specialty Diversified International

Fund	1-Year Total Return (%)	3-Year Annual Return (%)	5-Year Annual Return (%)
Janus Overseas	24.4	21.4	N/A
Janus Worldwide	21.4	21.1	19.1
Harbor International Growth	15.6	17.1	N/A
American Century International Discovery	23.4	17.0	N/A
Founders Worldwide Growth	9.5	15.3	13.4
Average for all funds in sector	12.7	9.6	11.2

The Top-Performing Mutual Funds,
Category 9: Taxable Income—Short/Intermediate Term

Fund	1-Year Total Return (%)	3-Year Annual Return (%)	5-Year Annual Return (%)
Fremont Bond	11.1	9.5	N/A
Vanguard Bond Index Long-Term	8.8	9.2	N/A
Harbor Bond	9.6	8.6	8.1
Warburg Pincus Fixed Income	9.3	8.4	7.8
Hotchkis & Wiley Low Duration	7.6	8.3	N/A
Average for all funds in sector	7.1	6.7	6.1

The Top-Performing Mutual Funds,
Category 10: Taxable Income—General

Fund	1-Year Total Return (%)	3-Year Annual Return (%)	5-Year Annual Return (%)
Northeast Investors Trust	16.5	13.7	14.6
Strong Corporate Bond	12.0	11.9	10.6
Nicholas Income	13.5	11.5	10.2
Vanguard Preferred Stock	12.6	11.4	9.2
Dreyfus Strategic Income	10.2	9.7	8.7
Average for all funds in sector	9.9	8.8	8.5

The Top-Performing Mutual Funds, Category 11: Taxable Income—World

Fund	1-Year Total Return (%)	3-Year Annual Return (%)	5-Year Annual Return (%)
Fidelity New Markets Income	40.1	20.6	N/A
Scudder Emerging Markets Income	29.6	19.4	N/A
Lazard Strategic Yield	12.9	10.4	9.2
Legg Mason Global Government	7.9	9.8	N/A
Warburg Pincus Global Fixed-Income	10.2	9.1	8.5
Average for all funds in sector	8.0	8.4	6.8

The Top-Performing Mutual Funds, Category 12: Tax-Free—Short/Intermediate Term

Fund	1-Year Total Return (%)	3-Year Annual Return (%)	5-Year Annual Return (%)
USAA Tax-Exempt Intermediate-Term	8.0	6.8	6.9
Fidelity Limited-Term Municipal	7.2	6.6	6.7
Vanguard Municipal Intermediate Return	6.7	6.2	6.9
Scudder Medium-Term Tax-Free	6.8	6.2	6.6
T. Rowe Price Tax-Free Insured	6.3	6.0	N/A
Average for all funds in sector	5.9	5.6	5.7

The Top-Performing Mutual Funds, Category 13: Tax-Free—General

Fund	1-Year Total Return (%)	3-Year Annual Return (%)	5-Year Annual Return (%)
Vanguard Municipal Long-Term	8.6	7.5	7.6
Safco Municipal Long-Term	9.0	7.4	7.1
Fidelity Spartan Municipal Income	8.2	7.2	7.0
SIT Tax-Free Income	8.2	7.2	7.1
Scudder Managed Municipal Bond	8.2	7.1	7.2
Average for all funds in sector	7.6	6.5	6.7

❖ THEN *and* NOW ❖

Number of Women in Congress

• • •

1947: 8

1996: 57

The Highest-Yielding Consumer-Oriented Money Market Funds of 1996

Fund Name	*Yield (%)*
Strong Heritage Money Fund	5.72
OLDE Premium Plus MM Series	5.68
E Fund	5.48
Kiewit Mutual Fund/MMP	5.40
Aetna Money Market Fund/CI A	5.38
Nations Prime Fund/Primary A	5.36
Transamerica Premier Cash Res/Inv	5.32
Strong Money Market Fund	5.31
Vanguard MMR/Prime/Retail Sh	5.29
Fremont Money Market Fund	5.28
Lake Forest Money Market Fund	5.28

The Largest Consumer-Oriented
Money Market Funds of 1996

Fund Name	Assets (billions of dollars)
Merrill Lynch CMA Money Fund	37.0
Smith Barney Cast Port/CI A	27.5
Vanguard MMR/Prime/Retail Sh	22.6
Fidelity Cash Reserves	21.7
Schwab Money Market Fund	18.1
Dean Witter/Liquid Asset Fund	12.0
Schwab Value Advantage MF	10.5
Fidelity Spartan MMF	9.1
Centennial Money Market Trust	8.1
Dean Witter/Active Assets MT	7.9

❖ THEN *and* NOW ❖

Percentage of the Population Age 25
and Over with a High School
Diploma/College Degree

• • •

1947: 33/5 percent

1993: 80/22 percent

The Ten Largest Bond Mutual Funds, as of December 31, 1995

Fund	Assets (millions of dollars)
Franklin CA Tax-Free Income I	13,555.9
Franklin U.S. Government Securities I	11,105.9
Dean Witter U.S. Government Securities	7,938.7
Franklin Federal Tax-Free Income I	7,210.6
Vanguard Fixed-Income GNMA	6,907.7
IDS High-Yield Tax-Exempt A	6,363.4
Bond Fund of America	6,290.2
Vanguard Municipal Bond Intermediate-Term	5,770.1
AARP GNMA & U.S. Treasury	5,257.3
Franklin NY Tax-Free Income I	4,861.4

The Top Ten Bond Funds: Municipal/National*

Fund	3-Year Average Net Return (%)	1-Year Average Net Return (%)
Blanchard Flexible Tax-Free Bond	6.0	5.9
Sit Tax-Free Income	5.6	6.9
Vanguard Municipal Long-Term Treasury	5.0	6.7
Vanguard Municipal High-Yield	4.9	6.0
Vanguard Municipal Insured Long-Term	4.9	6.3
USAA Tax-Exempt Intermediate-Term	4.9	5.3
1784 Tax-Exempt Medium-Term Income	4.8	5.0
Vanguard Municipal Intermediate-Term	4.8	4.8
Schwab Long-Term Tax-Free Bond	4.6	5.7
United Municipal High-Income A	4.5	3.0
Average for all funds in this category	3.3	2.5

*Performance is through October 1996 and is net of expenses and expected taxes.

The Top Ten Bond Funds: Corporate—High-Yield*

Fund	3-Year Average Net Return (%)	1-Year Average Net Return (%)
Northeast Investors Trust	10.2	15.5
Mainstay High-Yield Corporate Bond B	8.1	7.2
Value Line Aggressive Income	7.8	16.5
Seligman High-Yield Bond A	6.8	5.4
Fidelity Advisor High-Yield T	6.1	6.3
Columbia High-Yield	5.8	6.9
Nicholas Income	5.7	8.9
Federated High-Income Bond A	5.4	4.9
First Investors Fund for Income A	5.4	3.7
Vanguard F-1 High-Yield Corporate	5.2	5.1
Average for all funds in this category	4.3	6.7

*Performance is through October 1996 and is net of expenses and expected taxes.

❖ THEN *and* NOW ❖

Annual per-Pupil Expenditure
in the New York Public Schools

• • •

1947 average: $263
1947 average, adjusted for inflation: $1,940

1995 average: $8,300

The Top Ten Bond Funds:
Corporate—General*

Fund	3-Year Average Net Return (%)	1-Year Average Net Return (%)
Loomis Sayles Bond	8.9	11.3
CGM Fixed-Income	7.0	15.0
Strong Corporate Bond	6.5	5.9
T. Rowe Price Spectrum Income	5.3	6.9
Managers Bond	5.3	5.5
Vanguard Preferred Stock	4.7	5.9
Phoenix Multi-Sector S-T Bond A	4.3	6.4
Strong Advantage	4.1	4.5
Warburg Pincus Fixed-Income	4.1	4.9
Blanchard Short-Term Flexible Income	4.0	5.4
Average for all funds in this category	2.4	2.1

*Performance is through October 1996 and is net of expenses and expected taxes.

The Top Ten Bond Funds: Government—Treasury

Fund	3-Year Average Net Return (%)	1-Year Average Net Return (%)
Eaton Vance Short-Term Treasury	4.8	5.0
Permanent Portfolio Treasury Bill	3.6	3.5
Vanguard F-1 Short-Term U.S. Treasury	3.4	3.8
Aim Limited-Maturity Treasury Shares Retail	3.0	2.8
T. Rowe Price U.S. Treasury Intermediate	3.0	2.5
Vanguard F-1 Intermediate-Term U.S. Treasury	2.9	2.9
Benham Treasury Note	2.9	4.1
Columbia U.S. Government Securities	2.9	3.7
T. Rowe Price U.S. Treasury Long-Term	2.8	0.5
Warburg Pincus Intermediate-Maturity Government	2.8	3.3
Average for all funds in this category	2.0	1.7

Milestones of the
Dow Jones Industrial Average

First Close Over . . .	Date
100	January 12, 1906
500	March 12, 1956
1,000	November 14, 1972
2,000	January 8, 1987
3,000	April 17, 1991
4,000	February 23, 1995
5,000	November 21, 1995
6,000	October 14, 1996
7,000	February 13, 1997
8,000	July 16, 1997

❖ THEN *and* NOW ❖

Cost of a Top-Selling Car

• • •

1947 price: $1,220 (Chevrolet)
1947 price, adjusted for inflation: $8,990

1997 price: $18,545 (Ford Taurus)

Stocks in the Dow Jones Industrial Average

The Dow Jones Industrial Average is calculated using the returns of 30 established stocks listed on the New York Stock Exchange. Although this index incorporates the returns of only 30 of the thousands of publicly traded stocks in the United States, it is the most closely watched stock index in the world. Membership in this exclusive club, which undergoes occasional changes, is as follows:

Stock Name	Stock Symbol	Stock Name	Stock Symbol
Alcoa	AA	Hewlett-Packard	HWP
Allied Signal	ALD	IBM	IBM
American Express	AXP	International Paper	IP
AT&T	T	Johnson & Johnson	JNJ
Boeing	BA	McDonald's	MCD
Caterpillar	CAT	Merck	MRK
Chevron	CHV	Minnesota Mining (3M)	MMM
Coca-Cola	KO	J. P. Morgan	JPM
Disney	DIS	Philip Morris	MO
DuPont	DD	Procter & Gamble	PG
Eastman Kodak	EK	Sears Roebuck	S
Exxon	XON	Travelers Group	TRV
General Electric	GE	Union Carbide	UK
General Motors	GM	United Technologies	UTX
Goodyear	GT	Wal-Mart	WMT

Bernadette Murphy's List
of Pioneer Women on Wall Street

Women first arrived on Wall Street during World War I. Their role was to sell U.S. savings bonds to help fund the war effort and they were very good at their work—so good, in fact, that Mr. Dillon, of Dillon, Read & Co., suggested the women remain on Wall Street but turn their efforts to marketing securities other than savings bonds.

In 1921 five women formed the Women's Bond Club, which is still in existence today. The founding members were

> Mary Riis, Dillon, Read & Co.
> Elizabeth Cook, Hemphill Noyes & Co.
> Catherine Pepper, National City Bank
> Florence Bliss, Self-employed
> Louise Watson, Guaranty Co.

CATHERINE PEPPER was reputed to be the highest-paid woman on Wall Street in 1929.

ISABELLE BENHAM was an early member of the Women's Bond Club. She was recognized as the finest analyst of railroads in the investment industry and was a member of the investment banking division of R. W. Presspich & Co. The firm was considered the authority on the railroad industry. Ms. Benham was made a partner of R. W. Pressprich in 1965.

MURIEL SIEBERT joined the research department of Bache & Co. in 1954. She was assigned coverage of the airline industry and shortly after, the aerospace industry. She was the first woman analyst in both these industries. In 1967 she bought her own seat on the New York Stock Exchange and became the exchange's first woman member. In 1977 she was the first woman to be appointed superintendent of banking in New York State, a post she held until 1982, when she returned to Wall Street to once again assume leadership of her company, which carries her name.

In 1956, eight young Wall Street women became tired of being excluded from business luncheons when prominent speakers were the guests of honor. They decided to form the Young Women's Financial Association and invite their own guests to address the group. The founding members were

> Elizabeth Heaton (Mohr)
> Audrey Hochberg
> Nancy McNamara (Bentley)
> Susan Rappaport (Knafel)
> Jane Sheppard
> Gloria Swope (Marron)
> Joan Williams (Farr)
> Nancy Zuger

By the early 1970s, the organization had grown to 125 members and the name was changed to the Financial Women's Association. Today the association has more than a thousand members.

JOAN WILLIAMS FARR, of Oppenheimer & Co., a cosmetics and toiletries analyst, was the first woman to be included among the *Institutional Investors* All Star Team of analysts in 1972 and 1973. She is currently vice president of the Bank of New York.

JEAN RICHARDS and **MARJORIE JONES** were appointed vice presidents of White Weld & Co. on January 11, 1966. The media noted that "White Weld was virtually the first major, old line investment house to boost a woman to the upper executive level."

DORIS MAYDEN (BACHRACH) was a generalist as a security analyst because she was responsible for a number of industries. In January 1966 she became the first woman to be made a corporate officer of an investment company. She was appointed Corporate Secretary of General American Investors.

CAROL BALDI became the first woman to be made an officer of U.S. Trust Co. in 1961. She was made first vice president in 1968. In 1972 she became president of Lombard, Odier, Inc., in New York. Today she heads her own investment firm.

JANE L. BRETT (HOLT) of Walter B. Delafield & Co., a noted security analyst, was elected president of the New York Society of Security Analysts for 1967–68. She was the first woman to hold this position since its founding in 1937. The New York Society of Security Analysts is the largest individual society of analysts in America.

JULIA MONTGOMERY WALSH joined Ferris & Co. in 1954 as an account executive. She was elected to the board of directors of the American Stock Exchange for 1971–72. In the early 1970s she was also selected to be a regular panelist on *Wall $treet Week With Louis Rukeyser,* and in 1978 she bought her seat on the New York Stock Exchange. Her firm was named Julia Walsh & Sons. *Wall $treet Week With Louis Rukeyser* inducted her into its Hall of Fame on March 27, 1992.

A. MARION VAN DYKE (COOPER) became a chartered financial analyst in 1969. She was a portfolio manager in international equities for Bell Canada. She was president (1974–75) of the Montreal Society of Financial Analysts. Marion Van Dyke became the first woman to chair the Financial Analysts Federation (1979–80), an organization of analyst societies throughout the United States and Canada.

❖ **THEN** *and* **NOW** ❖

Percentage of Women Age 25
and Older in the Workforce

• • •

1948: 29.9 percent

1996: 58.7 percent

The Average Yield on 30-Year Treasury Bonds, 1977–1997

Year	Yield (%)
1977	7.75
1978	8.49
1979	9.28
1980	11.27
1981	13.45
1982	12.76
1983	11.18
1984	12.41
1985	10.79
1986	7.78
1987	8.59
1988	8.96
1989	8.45
1990	8.61
1991	8.14
1992	7.67
1993	6.59
1994	7.37
1995	6.88
1996	6.71
1997	6.90*

*As of June 1, 1997.

The Average Annual Yield on Long-Term AAA Corporate Bonds, 1977–1997

Year	Yield (%)
1976	8.43
1977	8.02
1978	8.73
1979	9.63
1980	11.94
1981	14.17
1982	13.79
1983	12.04
1984	12.71
1985	11.37
1986	9.02
1987	9.38
1988	9.71
1989	9.26
1990	9.32
1991	8.77
1992	8.14
1993	7.22
1994	7.97
1995	7.59
1996	7.37
1997	7.45*

*Through March 1997.

Julius Westheimer's
Ten Biggest Mistakes in the Market

MISTAKE 1:

In 1952, against my father's better judgment, I sold $125,000 worth of good stocks—AT&T, American Home Products, Standard Oil of New Jersey (now Exxon), General Electric, General Motors, IBM, Coca-Cola, etc.—and invested the money in our family-owned downtown Baltimore department store. When downtown deteriorated, and we didn't have the money or courage to open suburban branches, the store essentially folded and I lost almost everything. And just think where those stocks I sold would be now!

MISTAKE 2:

Around 1968, in Chicago, I asked some investment adviser, "What's the next Xerox?" (It had done spectacularly well at that time). He replied, "University Computing," so I invested $25,000 in that stock and virtually lost it all. Moral: Don't take curbstone advice.

MISTAKE 3:

In 1973, hypnotized by the "one-decision" (buy and hold forever) growth stock strategy, I put over half of what I was then worth in Texas Instruments, Polaroid, and Xerox. Each plunged more than 60 percent and I became a financial and emotional wreck (we can check the figures, but I don't think they ever recovered—at least not until long after I sold them at huge losses). Moral: Don't put all those eggs in one basket.

MISTAKE 4:

For two years on *Wall $treet Week With Louis Rukeyser*—between 1985 and autumn 1987—I predicted a bear market, but stocks continued to rise steadily. One week before the Crash of October 19, 1987, I delivered my famous mea culpa, confessing I had been too gloomy. A few days later the Dow Jones Industrial Average plunged 508 points in one day.

MISTAKE 5:

At what turned out to be the crest of the late-1980s real estate boom, I made my first investment in real estate—a limited partnership. This was some warehouse in New Jersey with "marvelous" occupancy prospects. I lost every nickel. They never got a tenant. Moral: Shoemaker, stick to your last!

MISTAKE 6:

After open-heart surgery in the spring of 1994, I saw the market plunging and, frightened by everything, sold 500 shares of Coca-Cola at $20 (adjusted for a split) and 500 shares of Merck at $30 (I was sure Hillary Clinton's health-care plan would doom the drug companies). At this writing Coke is selling at about $57 and Merck around $90. Westy, at then age 73, you should have known better!

MISTAKES 7–10:

In your next book, Lou.

Frank Cappiello's List of the Oldest Practicing Investment Advisers on Wall Street

Philip L. Carret: Carret & Company, New York City (born November 29, 1896)

Roy Neuberger: Neuberger & Berman, New York City (born July 21, 1903)

I. W. "Tubby" Burnham: Formerly with Drexel-Burnham, now runs a New York mutual fund (born January 7, 1909)

❖ THEN *and* NOW ❖

Price of a Gallon of Gas

• • •

1947: 23 cents
1947, adjusted for inflation: $1.70

1997: $1.22

The Favorite Countries
of United States Investors*

Nation	Invested in Nation's Stocks	Invested in Nation's Bonds	Total Invested
United Kingdom	142.1	440.0	582.1
Canada	21.8	189.4	211.2
Japan	71.7	64.3	136.0
France	11.5	18.7	30.2
Hong Kong	20.6	9.4	30.0
Germany	11.1	6.3	17.4
Mexico	7.8	5.7	13.5

*Based on 1995 purchases of bonds and stocks. All figures represent billions of dollars.

❖ THEN *and* NOW ❖

Median Home Price

• • •

1950: $7,350
1950, adjusted for inflation: $49,330

1996: $131,500

Elaine Garzarelli's
Favorite Legends of Wall Street

1. Mario Gabelli: Portfolio manager; charismatic and great stock picker.

2. Alan Greenspan: Economist with a wonderful knowledge of economic statistics.

3. Dick Hohenson: Economist at Donaldson, Lufkin & Jenrette; the best supply-side and demographic economist.

4. Ed Hyman: Economist at ISI; very creative and has the best daily information for institutional investors on current events.

5. Henry Kaufman: Economist who has great long-term insights and has moved markets.

6. Charles Maxwell: The best oil analyst I know, and extremely knowledgeable in many areas.

7. Muriel Siebert: The first woman to own a seat on the New York Stock Exchange, and a great business pioneer for all women.

8. John Templeton: He has a great philosophy of life and he's a giant mutual-fund pioneer.

9. Marty Zweig: A quiet star who is an amazing businessman and has an excellent combination of businesses.

10. Lou's dad, Merryle Stanley Rukeyser: The most entertaining and brilliant fellow ever.

Three-Month Treasury Bill Rates, Secondary Market, 1934–1997

Year	Rate (%)	Year	Rate (%)
1934	0.23	1966	4.96
1935	0.15	1967	4.97
1936	0.12	1968	5.96
1937	0.11	1969	7.82
1938	0.03	1970	4.87
1939	0.04	1971	4.01
1940	0.02	1972	5.07
1941	0.33	1973	7.45
1942	0.38	1974	7.15
1943	0.38	1975	5.44
1944	0.38	1976	4.35
1945	0.38	1977	6.07
1946	0.38	1978	9.08
1947	0.95	1979	12.04
1948	1.16	1980	15.49
1949	1.10	1981	10.85
1950	1.34	1982	7.94
1951	1.73	1983	9.00
1952	2.09	1984	8.06
1953	1.60	1985	7.10
1954	1.15	1986	5.53
1955	2.54	1987	5.77
1956	3.21	1988	8.07
1957	3.04	1989	7.63
1958	2.77	1990	6.74
1959	4.49	1991	4.07
1960	2.25	1992	3.22
1961	2.60	1993	3.06
1962	2.87	1994	5.60
1963	3.52	1995	5.14
1964	3.84	1996	4.99
1965	4.38	1997	5.05*

*As of June 1, 1997.

Six-Month Certificate of Deposit Yields, Secondary Market Rates, 1964–1997

Year	Yield (%)	Year	Yield (%)
1964	3.97	1981	16.09
1965	4.37	1982	14.66
1966	5.59	1983	9.45
1967	4.86	1984	11.96
1968	6.29	1985	7.58
1969	8.10	1986	6.72
1970	8.16	1987	7.15
1971	5.69	1988	7.69
1972	4.98	1989	9.09
1973	8.16	1990	8.28
1974	11.09	1991	6.26
1975	6.25	1992	3.97
1976	6.31	1993	3.36
1977	5.64	1994	4.85
1978	8.24	1995	5.80
1979	9.98	1996	5.64
1980	8.33	1997	5.87*

*As of June 1, 1997.

❖ THEN and NOW ❖

Percentage of Households
Owning Their Own Home

• • •

1950: 55 percent

1996: 65 percent

Bob Stovall's Super Bowl
Theory of Investing

The Super Bowl Investment Theory holds that the stock market will rise in any year an NFC or "old NFL" team wins the Super Bowl and will fall in any year an AFC team wins. (Several NFL teams—for example, the Cleveland Browns and Pittsburgh Steelers—were moved to the new AFC when the leagues merged after the 1969 season.) This theory has held every year since 1967, with the exceptions of 1970, 1978, and 1990.

Year	Dow Jones Industrial Average Close	Return (%)	Super Bowl Winner
1967	905.11	15.20	Green Bay (NFC)
1968	943.75	4.27	Green Bay (NFC)
1969	800.36	−15.19	N.Y. Jets (AFC)
1970	838.92	4.82	Kansas City (AFC)
1971	890.20	6.11	Baltimore (old NFL)
1972	1,020.02	14.58	Dallas (NFC)
1973	850.86	−16.58	Miami (AFC)
1974	616.24	−27.57	Miami (AFC)
1975	852.41	38.32	Pittsburgh (old NFL)
1976	1,004.65	17.86	Pittsburgh (old NFL)
1977	831.17	−17.27	Oakland (AFC)
1978	805.01	−3.15	Dallas (NFC)
1979	838.74	4.19	Pittsburgh (old NFL)
1980	963.99	14.93	Pittsburgh (old NFL)
1981	875.00	−9.23	Oakland (AFC)
1982	1,046.54	19.60	San Francisco (NFC)
1983	1,258.64	20.27	Washington (NFC)
1984	1,211.57	−3.74	L.A. Raiders (AFC)
1985	1,546.67	27.66	San Francisco (NFC)

Year	Dow Jones Industrial Average Close	Return (%)	Super Bowl Winner
1986	1,895.95	22.58	Chicago (NFC)
1987	1,938.83	2.26	N.Y. Giants (NFC)
1988	2,168.57	11.85	Washington (NFC)
1989	2,753.20	26.96	San Francisco (NFC)
1990	2,633.66	−4.34	San Francisco (NFC)
1991	3,168.83	20.32	N.Y. Giants (NFC)
1992	3,301.12	4.17	Washington (NFC)
1993	3,754.10	13.72	Dallas (NFC)
1994	3,834.44	2.14	Dallas (NFC)
1995	5,117.12	33.45	San Francisco (NFC)
1996	6,448.24	26.01	Dallas (NFC)
1997*	7,672.79	17.27	Green Bay (NFC)

*Through June 30, 1997.

❖ THEN *and* NOW ❖

Refrigerator

• • •

1947 price: $200 (9-cubic-foot model)
1947 price, adjusted for inflation: $1,470

1997 price: $700 (20-cubic-foot side-by-side model,
with ice maker)

Total Trading Volume of Registered United States Exchanges, 1980–1996*

Exchange	1980	1985	1990	1996
New York Stock Exchange	12,390	30,222	43,829	97,756
American Stock Exchange	1,659	2,115	3,125	4,300[†]
Midwest Stock Exchange	598	2,274	2,511	5,275
Pacific Stock Exchange	435	1,352	1,682	2,864

*In millions of dollars.
[†]1994 data.

❖ THEN *and* NOW ❖

Automatic Clothes Washer

• • •

1947 price: $240
1947 price, adjusted for inflation: $1,770

1997 price: $380

Charles R. Schwab's List of the Annual Return of the Dow Jones Industrial Average, 1930–1996

Returns calculated using holding-period return method.

Year	Open	Close	Return (%)
1930	248.48	164.58	−33.77
1931	164.58	77.90	−52.67
1932	77.90	59.93	−23.07
1933	59.93	99.90	66.69
1934	99.90	104.04	4.14
1935	104.04	144.13	38.53
1936	144.13	179.90	24.82
1937	179.90	120.85	−32.82
1938	120.85	154.76	28.06
1939	154.76	150.24	−2.92
1940	150.24	131.13	−12.72
1941	131.13	110.96	−15.38
1942	110.96	119.40	7.61
1943	119.40	135.89	13.81
1944	135.89	152.32	12.09
1945	152.32	192.91	26.65
1946	192.91	177.20	−8.14
1947	177.20	181.16	2.23
1948	181.16	177.30	−2.13
1949	177.30	200.13	12.88
1950	200.13	235.41	17.63
1951	235.41	269.23	14.37
1952	269.23	291.90	8.42
1953	291.90	280.90	−3.77
1954	280.90	404.39	43.96
1955	404.39	488.40	20.77

Year	Open	Close	Return (%)
1956	488.40	499.47	2.27
1957	499.47	435.69	−12.77
1958	435.69	583.65	33.96
1959	583.65	679.36	16.40
1960	679.36	615.89	−9.34
1961	615.89	731.14	18.71
1962	731.14	652.10	−10.81
1963	652.10	762.95	17.00
1964	762.95	874.13	14.57
1965	874.13	969.26	10.88
1966	969.26	785.69	−18.94
1967	785.69	905.11	15.20
1968	905.11	943.75	4.27
1969	943.75	800.36	−15.19
1970	800.36	838.92	4.82
1971	838.92	890.20	6.11
1972	890.20	1,020.02	14.58
1973	1,020.02	850.86	−16.58
1974	850.86	616.24	−27.57
1975	616.24	852.41	38.32
1976	852.41	1,004.65	17.86
1977	1,004.65	831.17	−17.27
1978	831.17	805.01	−3.15
1979	805.01	838.74	4.19
1980	838.74	963.99	14.93
1981	963.99	875.00	−9.23
1982	875.00	1,046.54	19.60
1983	1,046.54	1,258.64	20.27
1984	1,258.64	1,211.57	−3.74
1985	1,211.57	1,546.67	27.66
1986	1,546.67	1,895.95	22.58
1987	1,895.95	1,938.83	2.26
1988	1,938.83	2,168.57	11.85
1989	2,168.57	2,753.20	26.96

Year	Open	Close	Return (%)
1990	2,753.20	2,633.66	−4.34
1991	2,633.66	3,168.83	20.32
1992	3,168.83	3,301.12	4.17
1993	3,301.12	3,754.10	13.72
1994	3,754.10	3,834.44	2.14
1995	3,834.44	5,117.12	33.45
1996	5,117.12	6,448.24	26.01

❖ THEN *and* NOW ❖

Television

• • •

1947 price: $445 (12-inch black-and-white set)
1947 price, adjusted for inflation: $3,280

1997 price: $300 (25-inch color, with stereo sound)

Pete Colhoun's 13
Biggest Mistakes Investors Make

1. Thinking you can successfully "time" the market and know when to get out and when to get in.

2. Buying yesterday's favorites. Said another way—"investing through the rearview mirror."

3. Selling winners too soon. Let profits run.

4. Failing to take losses on mistakes and waiting to "get even to get out."

5. Owning too many items. Don't keep adding new, small holdings each year, especially in the same category.

6. Owning too many related items. Compile all your holdings (i.e., retirement assets, personal assets, etc.) and avoid overlap of industries.

7. Buying "hot" stocks because they sound exciting instead of because they meet stated investment objectives.

8. Making purchase or sale decisions based on where the price/share was sometime before. Relate stock prices to current/future events. Stock prices tend to overswing in both directions, rising too high when times are good and falling too low when times are bad.

9. Buying just for tax benefits and not for economic reasons. Beware of most tax shelters and don't put tax-exempt assets (e.g., municipal bonds) in tax-deferred accounts (e.g., retirement accounts).

10. Doing nothing. Don't let inertia or fear of getting the facts (regarding either your total account or an individual stock) lead you to squander opportunities. Don't let cash build to exorbitant levels in checking accounts.

11. Thinking that one guaranty covers all risks and you can't lose money. For example, a AAA-rated bond today may be a low-rated bond next week. Just because one eventually gets one's money back on a bond doesn't mean one can't lose money. Bond values go down if interest rates rise, and one must be alive at the maturity date to get face value.

12. Buying on a "cold call." It's foolish to send a check to a far-away brokerage firm for get-rich-quick schemes such as land drawings, gold-mine speculations, etc.

13. Thinking you are going to consistently beat the averages. Eighty percent of mutual funds don't beat their own bogey or benchmark over time. Fees associated with managed accounts (management fees, brokerage commissions, buy/sell spreads, trading functions, etc.) detract from gross performance.

❖ **THEN** *and* **NOW** ❖

Automatic Clothes Dryer

• • •

1947 price: $220
1947 price, adjusted for inflation: $1,620

1997 price: $270

PART

It's Your Money

Mary Farrell's List of Five Great Ways to Fund Your Child's Education

1. *Buy growth stocks or growth-stock mutual funds.* Stocks have historically been the best-performing asset over time, and if you start early, you reduce market timing risk and benefit from increasing earnings and dividends over time. Invest money every month as part of your budget.

2. *Benefit from the power of compounding.* Buy a mutual fund as soon as you know you're going to have a baby. As profits are reinvested and continue to grow, your nest egg multiplies. Assuming average returns of 10 percent a year in the stock market, $10,000 invested today should be worth over $67,000 in 20 years. (The past is no guarantee of future performance, of course.)

3. *Zero coupon bonds are a low-risk means of assuring future college funding.* When your child is born, buy government zero coupon bonds scheduled to mature in each of the years you need the tuition. At current interest rates, and assuming a 4 percent inflation rate in college tuition room and board, a $240,000 top-tier education for a newborn can be purchased for about $58,000. (See your accountant for exact tax advice on the expected income.)

4. *Consider moving to and establishing residence in a state with an outstanding state university system.* In-state residents can purchase a top-quality education at sometimes half the cost of private or Ivy League schools. North Carolina, Virginia, California, and Michigan are good examples of the many states with excellent state university systems.

5. *Enlist Grandma and Grandpa.* Annual tax-free gifts of $10,000 each to the child's account means $20,000 a year to invest for college. This can be good estate planning for grandparents because it avoids gift and estate taxes. They can also pay tuition directly to take advantage of the unlimited gift-tax exclusion available to pay for education expenses. Tax rates for estates over $600,000 rise rapidly, and with state taxes can quickly exceed 50 percent. Why not give it to the grandchildren instead of the government?

❖ THEN *and* NOW ❖

Half-Carat Diamond Ring at Galt's
in Washington, D.C.

• • •

1947 price: $525
1947 price, adjusted for inflation: $3,870

1997 price: $4,000

Attributes of 401(k) Plans
in the United States

Attribute	Percentage of Plans with Attribute
A 50 percent or larger matching employer contribution	55
Direct investment of employer contributions	65
Six or more investment options	45
No forfeiture of employer contributions	35
Daily account balance updates and fund transfers	36
Plan borrowing features	75
Administrative fees paid by employer	73
Phone transactions	75
Option of pretax or after-tax contributions	30
Rapid (within two weeks) delivery of monthly or quarterly statements	18

❖ THEN *and* NOW ❖

Percentage of Households
Owning a Television Set

• • •

1950: 9 percent

1995: 98 percent

Jim Jones's List of Unusual Taxes

1. *Convenience stores.* Under recent legislation, if you put gas pumps in front of your convenience store or fast-food joint, you might be eligible to depreciate the building over 15 years. If you don't have gas pumps, you have to depreciate the building over 39 years.

2. *Information returns from partnerships.* Partnerships are not required to provide their investors with K-1 forms, reporting their taxable income for the previous year, until April 15—the same day that the investor is supposed to file his or her tax return for the previous year.

3. *Electricity production credit for "closed-loop biomass."* You are eligible for a tax credit of 1.5 cents per kilowatt hour for electricity produced from "closed-loop biomass," which is defined as "any organic material from a plant which is planted exclusively for purposes of being used at a qualified facility to produce electricity."

4. *Independent-contractor status for newspaper boys.* They have special rules, but not other door-to-door salesmen.

5. *Moving a business.* If you completely leave a location and the land altogether, you can get certain tax benefits for the undepreciated costs. However, if you demolish a building and build a plant there that will eventually employ many people, the undepreciated costs get added to the cost of new plant, a much less favorable tax treatment.

6. *Children's income.* If a kid is under 14, his income is filed with his parents'. However, if the kid is 14 or older, then his income is taxed at its own rate. What is the magic of 14?

7. *Sports equipment.* A tax equal to 10 percent of the selling price is imposed on the sale of any article of sport-fishing equipment by the manufacturer, producer, or importer. A 3 percent tax rate is imposed for electric outboard motors and sonar devices suitable for finding fish. The latter are exempt in the case of (1) a graph recorder, (2) a digital type, (3) a meter readout, or (4) a combination graph recorder or combination meter readout, even if the fish images appear on such devices.

8. *Exclusions from income.* Volume cap—the state ceiling applicable under Section 146 of the 1986 Code for calendar year 1987 for the state that ratified the United States Constitution on May 29, 1790, shall be $150,000,000 higher than the state ceiling otherwise applicable under such section for such a year.

9. *Estates.* When a person dies and leaves an estate, the estate must get a new TIN (taxpayer identification number) from the one the person had.

10. *Rental of vacation homes.* If you rent your vacation home for 14 days, there is no tax on the income. If you rent for 15 days or more, it is all taxable income.

❖ THEN *and* NOW ❖

Basic Local Monthly Phone Service
in St. Louis, Private Line

• • •

1947 cost: $5.50
1947 cost, adjusted for inflation: $40.50

1997 cost: $11.40

States with the Highest
General Sales Tax Rates in 1996

State	Sales Tax (%)
Mississippi	7.00
Rhode Island	7.00
Minnesota	6.50
Nevada	6.50
Washington	6.50
Illinois	6.25
Texas	6.25
California	6.00
Connecticut	6.00
Florida	6.00
Kentucky	6.00
Maine	6.00
Michigan	6.00
New Jersey	6.00
Pennsylvania	6.00
Tennessee	6.00
West Virginia	6.00

❖ THEN *and* NOW ❖

Three-Minute Phone Call,
New York to Los Angeles

• • •

1947 cost: $2.50
1947 cost, adjusted for inflation: $18.40

1997 cost: 45 cents

States Without a
General Sales Tax in 1996

Alaska
Delaware
Montana
New Hampshire
Oregon

States Without a
State Income Tax in 1996

Alaska
Florida
Nevada
South Dakota
Texas
Washington
Wyoming

The History of Tax Freedom Day

Tax Freedom Day occurs on the date the average American has earned enough in the year to pay all annual federal, state, and local tax obligations.

Year	Date
1970	April 26
1975	April 27
1980	May 1
1985	April 30
1990	May 3
1991	May 2
1992	May 1
1993	May 3
1994	May 5
1995	May 6
1996	May 7
1997	May 9

The Typical Dollar Value (for Income Tax Purposes) of Donated Goods

Item	Good Condition	Fair Condition
Man's cardigan sweater	$ 15	$10
Man's two-piece dress suit	70	40
Man's ski jacket	35	25
Woman's long-sleeved blouse	15	9
Woman's formal dress (short)	60	35
Woman's raincoat	20	16
Boy's casual jacket	10	8
Girl's jumper	12	9
Infant's snowsuit	12	8
Upright vacuum cleaner	65	22
Computerized exercise bike	250	70
Catcher's glove	65	30
Baby's playpen	30	20
Color console TV	160	60

❖ THEN *and* NOW ❖

A Pair of Stockings

•   •   •

1947 price: $10
1947 price, adjusted for inflation: $74

1997 price: $4 (pantyhose)

Your Risk of Being Audited
by the Internal Revenue Service

Type of Return	Percentage Audited
PERSONAL	
Income under $100,000	0.83
Income over $100,000	2.94
SELF-EMPLOYED	
Gross revenue under $100,000	3.64
Gross revenue over $100,000	3.57
FARMERS	
Gross revenue under $100,000	1.16
Gross revenue over $100,000	1.74
ESTATES	
Assets under $1 million	8.20
Assets $1 million to $5 million	22.78
Assets over $5 million	48.00

United States Bank Credit Card
Lending to Individuals, 1976–1996*

Year	Lending (billions of dollars)
1976	14.4
1977	18.5
1978	24.4
1979	29.9
1980	29.9
1981	32.8
1982	36.7
1983	45.2
1984	61.2
1985	78.4
1986	91.9
1987	102.9
1988	117.2
1989	131.5
1990	133.6
1991	139.1
1992	135.9
1993	153.5
1994	186.8
1995	215.8
1996	231.4

*Lending by insured commercial banks for "credit card and related plans."

FDIC Deposit Insurance Coverage, per Account, 1934–1996

Year	Insurance Coverage
1934*	$ 2,500
1934–49	5,000
1950–65	10,000
1966–68	15,000
1969–73	20,000
1974–79	40,000
1980–present	100,000

*From January 1 to June 30.

❖ THEN *and* NOW ❖

New York City Subway Fare

• • •

1947: 10 cents
1947, adjusted for inflation: 75 cents

1997: $1.50

Financing Your Retirement

How far will your savings go? The table shows the amount needed to provide $100 in monthly income during retirement at various interest rates.

Years in Retirement	4 Percent	6 Percent	8 Percent	10 Percent	12 Percent
25	$26,300	$21,200	$17,400	$14,600	$12,500
30	30,800	23,900	19,000	15,600	13,100
35	35,200	26,200	20,300	16,300	13,500
40	39,300	28,200	21,300	16,800	13,700

❖ THEN *and* NOW ❖

Brooks Brothers Gray Flannel Suit

• • •

1947 price: $70
1947 price, adjusted for inflation: $520

1997 price: $598

Annual Social Security Survivor's Benefits

Worker's Age at Death	Family Profile	Benefit with Annual Earnings of $30,000	Benefit with Annual Earnings of $60,000
35	Spouse and one child	$19,000	$25,800
	Spouse and two or more children	22,100	30,100
	Spouse at age 60	9,000	12,300
45	Spouse and one child	$19,000	$25,000
	Spouse and two or more children	22,100	29,100
	Spouse at age 60	9,000	11,900
55	Spouse and one child	$18,900	$23,400
	Spouse and two or more children	22,100	27,200
	Spouse at age 60	9,000	11,100

Pete Colhoun's Five
Most Important Documents to Have

1. *A will.* To determine where your assets go at death. Seventy percent of people don't have one.

2. *A living will.* To authorize someone to make decisions affecting your life if you can't.

3. *A power of attorney.* To authorize someone to manage your finances if you are sick or disabled.

4. *A directory of basic information.* To inform your executor or authorized power of attorney what assets you own (stocks, bonds, loan agreements, retirement funds, real estate, mutual funds, etc.), where they are located (safe-deposit box, with current or former employer, what registration, etc.), their approximate value, and the names of your professional advisers (tax advisers, lawyers, investment counselors, trustees, etc.).

5. *Updated year-end statement.* To update yourself and anyone helping with your estate planning, investment planning, or record keeping. The statements should list all assets, current value (even if estimated), tax cost basis, current income, and last year's performance. The assets should be divided into broad asset categories—such as stocks, bonds, real estate, cash—and, ideally, subcategories such as domestic stocks, international stocks, small and large, etc.

Local Tax Burdens

The table shows United States cities with populations of 200,000 or more, ranked by per capita local tax burden.

Rank	City	City Government Taxes per Capita, 1991
1	Washington, D.C.	$3,978
2	New York City	2,190
3	San Francisco	1,302
4	Richmond	1,292
5	Boston	1,063
6	Philadelphia	1,016
7	Nashville-Davidson, Tenn.	947
8	Baltimore	902
9	Virginia Beach, Va.	884
10	Denver	829
11	Norfolk, Va.	797
12	Anchorage	793
13	Kansas City, Mo.	755
14	St. Louis, Mo.	692
15	Seattle	657
16	Pittsburgh	646
17	Cincinnati	615
18	New Orleans	604
19	Chicago	573
20	Oakland, Calif.	571
21	Rochester, N.Y.	568
22	Atlanta	552
23	Birmingham, Ala.	547
24	Cleveland	545
25	Indianapolis	536
26	Louisville, Ky.	534
27	Los Angeles	532

Rank	City	City Government Taxes per Capita, 1991
28	Minneapolis	522
29	Honolulu*	521
30	Detroit	513
31	Portland, Oreg.	501
32	Baton Rouge†	499
33	Dallas	490
34	Mobile, Ala.	486
35	Miami	464
36	Lexington-Fayette, Ky.	450
37	Fort Worth	448
38	Tulsa	446
39	Tampa	441
40	Houston	440
41	Columbus, Ohio	428
42	Sacramento	426
42	Jersey City, N.J.	426
44	Akron, Ohio	415
44	Oklahoma City	415
46	San Jose, Calif.	413
47	Omaha	411
48	Anaheim, Calif.	409
49	Buffalo, N.Y.	404
50	Aurora, Colo.	396
51	Jacksonville, Fla.	380
52	Toledo, Ohio	377
53	St. Petersburg	376
54	Austin	374
54	Long Beach, Calif.	374
56	Raleigh, N.C.	359
56	Charlotte, N.C.	359
58	St. Paul	343

*Data are for Honolulu City/County.
†Data are for East Baton Rouge Parish.

Rank	City	City Government Taxes per Capita, 1991
59	Santa Ana, Calif.	338
60	San Diego	335
60	Phoenix	335
62	Arlington, Tex.	331
62	Tucson	331
64	Riverside, Calif.	328
64	Albuquerque	328
66	Newark	318
67	Stockton, Calif.	307
68	Fresno, Calif.	305
69	Colorado Springs	300
70	Corpus Christi, Tex.	263
71	Milwaukee	255
72	Memphis	251
73	Wichita	249
74	El Paso	234
75	Las Vegas	229
76	San Antonio	221
77	Mesa, Ariz.	158

How to Become a Millionaire

How much do you need to invest annually to accumulate $1,000,000 by age 65?*

Age You Begin Investing	Required Annual Contribution If Fund Earns 6% (dollars)	Required Annual Contribution If Fund Earns 11% (dollars)
22	5,006	1,126
25	6,059	1,546
30	8,395	2,630
35	11,792	4,506
40	16,904	7,813
45	25,005	13,838
50	38,952	25,517
55	66,793	51,121
60	143,363	126,377

*Assumes final contribution made on your sixty-fifth birthday.

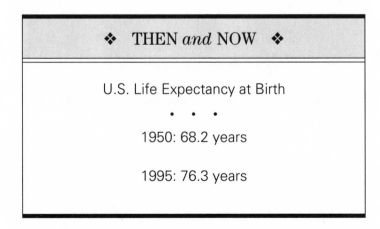

❖ THEN *and* NOW ❖

U.S. Life Expectancy at Birth

• • •

1950: 68.2 years

1995: 76.3 years

The Net Worth of United States Families*

	Percentage of Families		
Net Worth	1989	1992	1995
Less than $10,000	27.8	27.0	25.8
$10,000–$24,999	9.3	10.4	10.0
$25,000–$49,999	10.1	11.4	11.6
$50,000–$99,999	14.6	15.3	16.9
$100,000–$249,999	21.6	20.7	21.3
$250,000 and more	16.5	15.2	14.4

*In 1995 dollars.

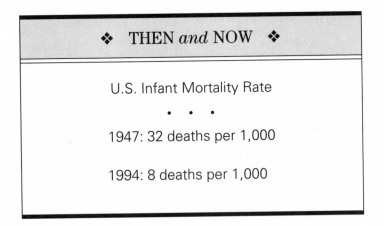

❖ THEN and NOW ❖

U.S. Infant Mortality Rate

•   •   •

1947: 32 deaths per 1,000

1994: 8 deaths per 1,000

Fortune's 15 Best Cities in the United States to Work and Raise a Family

Rank	City
1	Seattle
2	Denver
3	Philadelphia
4	Minneapolis
5	Raleigh-Durham
6	St. Louis
7	Cincinnati
8	Washington
9	Pittsburgh
10	Dallas–Fort Worth
11	Atlanta
12	Baltimore
13	Boston
14	Milwaukee
15	Nashville

❖ THEN *and* NOW ❖

Amount Spent on Dental Care
in United States

• • •

1947: $783 million
1947, adjusted for inflation: $5.8 billion

1994: $42.2 billion

Tips on Tipping

Airport shuttle or courtesy van driver	$1, $2 if luggage assistance provided
Airport baggage handler	$3 plus $1 per bag
Bartender	15% of tab
Bellhop, baggage assistance	$2 per bag
Bellhop, special tasks (e.g., ice, messages)	$2 per task
Hotel concierge, special service	$5
Hotel doorman assistance	$1
Hotel doorman (baggage storage)	$1 per bag
Hotel housekeeper	$2 per day
Hotel room service	20% of bill
Newspaper delivery person	$10–$20 annually
Pizza delivery person	20% of bill
Postal carrier	$25 annually
Restaurant coat or hat check person	$1 per item
Restaurant parking attendant	$2
Restaurant waiter	15% of bill
Shoe-shine person	$1

Median Household Income, by State

State (or D.C.)	1990 Rank	1990 Median Household Income	1994 Rank	1994 Median Household Income
United States	*	$33,952	*	$32,264
New Hampshire	1	46,269	16	35,245
Alaska	2	44,560	1	45,367
Hawaii	3	44,132	3	42,255
Connecticut	4	44,074	4	41,097
Maryland	5	44,060	6	39,198
New Jersey	6	43,920	2	42,280
Massachusetts	7	41,100	5	40,500
Virginia	8	39,769	8	37,647
California	9	37,747	14	35,331
Illinois	10	36,899	17	35,081
Washington	11	36,412	19	33,533
Nevada	12	36,311	10	35,871
Rhode Island	13	36,248	23	31,928
New York	14	35,821	24	31,899
Minnesota	15	35,678	18	33,644
Vermont	16	35,262	11	35,802
Delaware	17	34,928	9	35,873
Colorado	18	34,848	7	37,833
Wisconsin	19	34,823	13	35,388
Utah	20	34,178	12	35,716
Ohio	21	34,032	25	31,855
Michigan	22	33,945	15	35,284
Kansas	23	33,923	39	28,322
Wyoming	24	33,405	20	33,140
Oregon	25	33,202	29	31,456

*Not applicable.

State (or D.C.)	1990 Rank	1990 Median Household Income	1994 Rank	1994 Median Household Income
Arizona	26	$33,137	30	$31,293
Pennsylvania	27	32,889	22	32,066
South Carolina	28	32,582	35	29,846
Texas	29	32,008	31	30,755
Georgia	30	31,251	28	31,467
Nebraska	31	31,162	26	31,794
Maine	32	31,141	32	30,316
District of Columbia	*	31,060	*	30,116
Missouri	33	30,992	33	30,190
Iowa	34	30,942	21	33,079
Indiana	35	30,533	41	27,858
Florida	36	30,258	37	29,294
North Carolina	37	29,854	34	30,114
Idaho	38	28,693	27	31,536
North Dakota	39	28,647	40	28,278
New Mexico	40	28,392	45	26,905
Kentucky	41	28,098	46	26,595
South Dakota	42	27,861	36	29,733
Oklahoma	43	27,649	44	26,991
Montana	44	26,505	42	27,631
Alabama	45	26,484	43	27,196
Arkansas	46	25,837	48	25,565
Tennessee	47	25,617	38	28,639
Louisiana	48	25,405	47	25,676
West Virginia	49	25,101	50	23,564
Mississippi	50	22,880	49	25,400

*Not applicable.

Family-Held Investments in the United States, by Age of the Head of Household

Age of Head of Household	Percent Owning Bonds		Percent Owning Stocks		Percent Owning Mutual Funds	
	1992	1995	1992	1995	1992	1995
Younger than 35	1.4	0.5	10.7	11.1	5.2	8.8
35–44	2.6	1.6	19.4	14.5	10.0	10.5
45–54	5.4	4.6	18.6	17.5	9.4	16.0
55–64	4.8	2.9	21.6	14.9	15.9	15.2
65–74	7.5	5.1	16.0	18.0	14.1	13.7
75 or older	8.5	7.0	19.2	21.3	14.3	10.4

❖ THEN *and* NOW ❖

One Day in the Intensive-Care Unit
at Yale–New Haven Hospital

• • •

1947 cost: $35
1947 cost, adjusted for inflation: $260

1996 cost: $2,300

Family Debt

The table shows the percentage of families with debt payments sixty or more days past due, by age of head of household.

Age of Head of Household	1989 (%)	1992 (%)	1995 (%)
Younger than 35	10.8	8.2	8.8
35–44	5.9	7.0	7.4
45–54	4.6	5.4	7.8
55–64	7.5	4.6	2.5
65–74	3.3	1.1	5.0
75 or older	1.1	2.1	4.2

❖ **THEN** *and* **NOW** ❖

Percent of Workers Covered
by a Retirement Plan

• • •

1945: 19 percent

1992: 46 percent

Knight Kiplinger's Eight Keys to Financial Security

KEY 1: INVEST IN YOURSELF.

Your own earning power is the greatest asset you'll ever have. Keep it strong through continuous education, training, and personal growth. Pay close attention to your physical and spiritual health. And as you accumulate financial assets, study techniques of sound money management as carefully as you learned your career skills.

KEY 2: PROTECT YOUR LOVED ONES AND YOUR ASSETS.

Before you acquire any financial assets, make sure you have enough insurance against life's big risks: illness, disability, liability, and early death. How much coverage is enough? Ask the professionals, and don't be surprised if the figures are much more than you have now, or think you need. When an emergency arises, you—or your beneficiaries—won't regret having too much insurance.

KEY 3: BORROW SPARINGLY.

Use credit only to purchase things of lasting value: a home, education, and job training—maybe a car. Pay cash for everything else: clothing, travel, entertainment, general living expenses. (Know anyone who got into big financial trouble because they *didn't* borrow money? I don't.)

KEY 4: PAY YOURSELF FIRST.

This old adage—which means saving a fixed portion of your earnings each month, rain or shine, along with paying your other bills—really works, and the opposite doesn't. It entails budgeting regular deposits to your mutual fund, CDs, brokerage account, payroll savings plan, whatever, just as you pay your monthly rent, mortgage, auto loan, or tuition repayment. If you don't, your discretionary expenses will have a magical way of expanding to consume all available funds—*before* you get around to saving or investing.

KEY 5: DON'T GO FOR THE HOME RUNS.

In investing, as in baseball, those who swing for the fences get some home runs, but they also strike out a lot, and their batting averages— average annual total returns—reflect it. Most successful investors aim for lots of singles and doubles, and like most journeymen hitters, they get the occasional homer too.

They don't engage in market timing, because most people can't catch market peaks and valleys accurately. They use dollar cost averaging to make sure they're in the market for the major moves, even if that means suffering through the occasional bear market.

KEY 6: INVEST IN QUALITY ASSETS OF DIVERSE TYPES.

When it comes time to get liquid—sell what you own—it will be a lot easier if you own assets perceived by markets to be things of quality. This applies to any kind of assets . . . U.S. stocks, bonds, real estate, foreign securities, even collectibles (which aren't investments but sometimes act like them).

The reason for balancing your wealth among different classes of assets is quite simple: at any particular time, some will enjoy the high prices of market favor, while others will be shunned by buyers, wisely or not. With diversity you hedge your bets, and when you need to sell, you won't have to dump temporarily depressed assets.

KEY 7: FUND A COMFORTABLE FUTURE WITH SIMPLER LIVING TODAY.

If you're not funding your tax-deferred IRA, 401(k), or other retirement plans to the maximum, it might be because everything you earn is going into big mortgage payments, auto lease payments, and credit card bills. Don't fret about the future; take steps now to make it comfortable for you and your heirs. Take a look at how you're living and try to decide what's important and what's dispensable.

KEY 8: GIVE GENEROUSLY TO CREATE A BETTER WORLD.

Your own financial security depends far more than you may think on the financial, physical, and spiritual well-being of others in your community and your nation. When you share your good fortune (your income and your wealth) by donating to education, medical charities, social service agencies, and the arts, you help create a stronger economy and a healthier, safer world.

❖ **THEN** *and* **NOW** ❖

Average Monthly Social Security Check

• • •

1947: $30
1947, adjusted for inflation: $220

1996: $720

Who's on That Bill?
Portraits on U.S. Currency

Denomination	Portrait
$1	George Washington
$2	Thomas Jefferson
$5	Abraham Lincoln
$10	Alexander Hamilton
$20	Andrew Jackson
$50	Ulysses S. Grant
$100	Benjamin Franklin
$500	William McKinley
$1,000	Grover Cleveland
$5,000	James Madison
$10,000	Salmon Chase
$100,000	Woodrow Wilson

❖ THEN *and* NOW ❖

One Round of Golf at Pebble Beach

• • •

1947 cost: $2
1947 cost, adjusted for inflation: $15

1997 cost: $225

Growth in Individual
Retirement Accounts, 1974–1997

The annual growth in individual retirement account investments
between 1974 and 1996 was 27.9 percent.

Year	Total IRA Investments (billions of dollars)	Year	Total IRA Investments (billions of dollars)
1974	1.5	1986	183.4
1975	2.5	1987	212.6
1976	5.1	1988	241.0
1977	7.9	1989	275.4
1978	12.5	1990	308.3
1979	17.6	1991	324.8
1980	22.0	1992	319.9
1981	29.4	1993	312.7
1982	51.0	1994	314.5
1983	76.9	1995	336.1
1984	110.8	1996	336.7
1985	149.3	1997*	337.3

*As of June 1, 1997.

The Cost of Higher Education, 1964–1996*

	Total Costs (U.S. dollars)	
School Year	Private Schools	Public Schools
1964–65	1,907	950
1965–66	2,005	983
1966–67	2,124	1,026
1967–68	2,205	1,064
1968–69	2,321	1,117
1969–70	2,530	1,203
1970–71	2,738	1,287
1971–72	2,917	1,357
1972–73	3,038	1,458
1973–74	3,164	1,517
1974–75	3,403	1,563
1975–76	3,663	1,666
1976–77	3,906	1,789
1977–78	4,158	1,888
1978–79	4,514	1,994
1979–80	4,912	2,165
1980–81	5,470	2,373
1981–82	6,166	2,663
1982–83	6,920	2,945
1983–84	7,508	3,156
1984–85	8,202	3,408
1985–86	8,885	3,571
1986–87	9,676	3,805
1987–88	10,512	4,050
1988–89	11,189	4,274
1989–90	12,018	4,504

* Undergraduate tuition, room, and board.

| School Year | Total Costs (U.S. dollars) | |
	Private Schools	Public Schools
1990–91	12,910	4,757
1991–92	13,907	5,135
1992–93	14,634	5,379
1993–94	15,496	5,694
1994–95	16,207	5,965
1995–96	17,207	6,252

❖ THEN *and* NOW ❖

Ticket to a Yankees Game, Lower Box Seat

• • •

1947 price: $2.50
1947 price, adjusted for inflation: $18

1996 price: $19

The 100 Largest U.S. Metropolitan Areas, Ranked by Housing Costs

City (or County)	1996 Median Price (dollars)	1996 Change (%)	1997 Forecast from 1996 (%)
United States	117,900	4.4	3.1
1. Honolulu	334,693	−7.5	−1.1
2. San Francisco	259,867	2.7	3.5
3. San Jose, Calif.	225,955	−0.1	0.6
4. Orange County, Calif.	209,859	−0.3	1.4
5. Bergen and Passaic Counties, N.J.	200,390	1.2	2.0
6. Newark, N.J.	194,380	1.6	1.8
7. Boston	191,491	5.4	3.0
8. Los Angeles	178,059	−1.3	−0.2
9. New York City	177,675	1.0	1.2
10. Middlesex, N.J.	175,056	1.4	2.7
11. San Diego	174,115	−0.8	0.5
12. Nassau and Suffolk Counties, N.Y.	163,464	−0.1	0.9
13. Washington, D.C.	159,761	−1.3	−0.9
14. Chicago	152,216	4.5	3.2
15. Ventura, Calif.	149,373	−1.1	0.6
16. Monmouth and Ocean Counties, N.J.	147,073	4.2	4.4
17. Seattle	145,741	−1.2	−0.4
18. Wilmington, Del.	138,489	3.8	3.2
19. Bakersfield, Calif.	137,585	1.2	3.4
20. New Haven	135,868	0.9	1.3
21. Hartford	132,012	−0.7	0.8
22. Denver	131,792	5.8	4.5
23. Portland, Oreg.	129,170	6.6	7.7

City (or County)	1996 Median Price (dollars)	1996 Change (%)	1997 Forecast from 1996 (%)
24. Riverside, Calif.	127,037	0.3	1.3
25. Raleigh-Durham	126,850	5.6	5.7
26. West Palm Beach, Fla.	125,536	4.8	4.2
27. Tacoma	124,126	2.6	1.8
28. Sacramento	123,563	0.1	0.3
29. Las Vegas	123,547	6.2	5.8
30. Albuquerque	122,867	6.2	5.2
31. Salt Lake City	121,685	13.5	5.4
32. Milwaukee	120,602	5.5	2.0
33. Philadelphia	117,533	2.7	1.1
34. Providence	117,200	0.8	1.7
35. Colorado Springs	115,836	5.9	5.9
36. Baltimore	115,432	−1.3	−0.1
37. Charlotte, N.C.	114,322	9.4	1.9
38. Vallejo, Calif.	113,860	3.6	3.1
39. Miami	111,640	4.9	4.6
40. Fort Lauderdale	111,515	3.8	3.5
41. Austin	111,327	8.6	4.8
42. Minneapolis–St. Paul	110,890	5.7	4.8
43. Norfolk, Va.	110,250	−1.0	1.4
44. Fresno, Calif.	109,595	2.3	3.9
45. Greensboro, N.C.	109,229	8.6	5.1
46. Birmingham, Ala.	107,766	3.7	3.4
47. Springfield, Mass.	106,571	−1.3	−0.4
48. Nashville	106,151	5.7	6.0
49. Albany	106,106	−6.5	−0.7
50. Cincinnati	104,965	5.3	2.9
51. Dallas	104,751	6.5	3.9
52. Columbus, Ohio	103,913	5.7	5.8
53. Sarasota, Fla.	103,380	4.3	1.2
54. Stockton, Calif.	100,652	2.2	2.9
55. Indianapolis	99,600	3.8	1.6

City (or County)	1996 Median Price (dollars)	1996 Change (%)	1997 Forecast from 1996 (%)
56. Atlanta	98,941	4.4	5.3
57. Ann Arbor, Mich.	98,534	2.6	3.2
58. Phoenix	98,533	4.3	4.1
59. Cleveland	96,629	0.9	0.8
60. Memphis	96,211	10.5	4.7
61. Charleston, S.C.	95,526	4.4	2.2
62. Richmond	95,195	0.3	1.2
63. Kansas City, Mo.	94,841	4.2	1.3
64. Knoxville, Tenn.	94,578	2.6	2.6
65. Orlando	93,777	1.3	1.1
66. Gary, Ind.	93,755	4.4	3.5
67. Greenville, S.C.	93,423	5.1	5.5
68. Fort Wayne, Ind.	91,802	5.4	3.6
69. Columbia, S.C.	91,710	6.8	1.8
70. St. Louis, Mo.	89,030	2.2	1.9
71. Akron	88,470	4.6	4.6
72. Jacksonville, Fla.	87,837	3.0	1.7
73. Jersey City	87,828	0.5	0.7
74. Dayton, Ohio	86,494	0.3	0.6
75. Allentown, Pa.	86,346	1.4	0.1
76. Rochester, N.Y.	85,644	−1.9	0.5
77. Buffalo	84,918	−0.1	−0.2
78. Pittsburgh	84,915	2.6	1.0
79. Houston	84,184	2.6	2.9
80. Louisville, Ky.	84,046	2.1	1.9
81. San Antonio	83,947	5.6	1.7
82. Detroit	83,912	−0.8	0.2
83. Tucson	83,337	2.7	2.2
84. Baton Rouge	83,282	3.0	2.1
85. Grand Rapids	82,209	5.1	4.1
86. Omaha	82,009	5.1	2.4
87. Harrisburg, Pa.	81,899	2.4	2.1

City (or County)	1996 Median Price (dollars)	1996 Change (%)	1997 Forecast from 1996 (%)
88. New Orleans	80,310	3.0	2.3
89. Wichita	80,258	5.9	5.4
90. Syracuse	79,981	−3.0	−1.6
91. El Paso	78,844	2.1	1.3
92. Tampa	78,145	−0.1	−0.3
93. Toledo	76,607	2.0	1.7
94. Little Rock	75,644	2.7	1.4
95. Scranton	75,422	2.7	1.3
96. Mobile	75,143	5.4	6.2
97. Oklahoma City	73,189	5.1	3.2
98. Youngstown, Ohio	71,012	5.4	1.7
99. Tulsa	70,495	6.3	3.6
100. McAllen, Tex.	60,905	2.0	1.6

❖ THEN *and* NOW ❖

Price of a Record Album/CD

• • •

1947: $1 to $3 (for Al Jolson record album)
1947, adjusted for inflation: $7 to $22

1997: $17 (for Hootie and the Blowfish CD)

Average Annual Pay, by State

When states share the same rank, the next-lower rank is omitted. Because of rounded-off data, states may show identical values but different ranks.

State (or D.C.)	1990 Rank	1990 Pay	1994 Rank	1994 Pay
United States	*	$23,602	*	$26,939
District of Columbia	*	33,717	*	40,919
Alaska	1	29,946	4	32,657
Connecticut	2	28,995	1	33,811
New York	3	28,873	2	33,439
New Jersey	4	28,449	2	33,439
Massachusetts	5	26,699	5	31,024
California	6	26,180	6	29,878
Michigan	7	25,376	7	29,541
Illinois	8	25,312	8	29,107
Maryland	9	24,730	9	28,416
Delaware	10	24,423	10	27,952
Pennsylvania	11	23,457	11	26,950
Hawaii	12	23,167	12	26,746
Minnesota	13	23,121	13	26,422
Colorado	14	22,908	15	26,155
Ohio	15	22,844	16	26,134
Virginia	16	22,750	17	26,035
Texas	17	22,700	18	25,959
Washington	18	22,646	14	26,362
New Hampshire	19	22,609	20	25,555
Rhode Island	20	22,388	21	25,454

*Not applicable.

State (or D.C.)	1990 Rank	1990 Pay	1994 Rank	1994 Pay
Nevada	21	$22,358	19	$25,700
Georgia	22	22,115	22	25,313
Missouri	23	21,716	25	24,628
Indiana	24	21,699	23	24,908
Arizona	25	21,443	27	24,276
Oregon	26	21,332	24	24,780
Wisconsin	27	21,101	26	24,324
Florida	28	21,030	29	23,918
West Virginia	29	20,715	34	22,959
Louisiana	30	20,646	32	23,178
Tennessee	31	20,611	28	24,106
Vermont	32	20,532	33	22,964
Alabama	33	20,468	30	23,616
Oklahoma	34	20,288	41	22,293
Kansas	35	20,238	35	22,907
North Carolina	36	20,220	31	23,460
Maine	37	20,154	39	22,389
Utah	38	20,074	36	22,811
Wyoming	39	20,049	43	22,054
Kentucky	40	19,947	37	22,747
South Carolina	41	19,668	38	22,477
New Mexico	42	19,347	40	22,351
Iowa	43	19,224	42	22,189
Idaho	44	18,991	44	21,938
Nebraska	45	18,577	45	21,500
Arkansas	46	18,204	46	20,898
Montana	47	17,895	48	20,218
Mississippi	48	17,718	47	20,382
North Dakota	49	17,626	49	19,893
South Dakota	50	16,430	50	19,255

The Consumer Price Index, 1961–1997

Year	Index	Year	Index
1961	89.6	1979	217.4
1962	90.6	1980	246.8
1963	91.7	1981	272.4
1964	92.9	1982	289.1
1965	94.5	1983	298.4
1966	97.2	1984	311.1
1967	100.0	1985	322.2
1968	104.2	1986	328.4
1969	109.8	1987	340.4
1970	116.3	1988	354.3
1971	121.3	1989	371.3
1972	125.3	1990	391.4
1973	133.1	1991	408.0
1974	147.7	1992	420.3
1975	161.2	1993	432.7
1976	170.5	1994	444.0
1977	181.5	1995	456.5
1978	195.4	1996	469.9
		1997*	479.6

*Estimated as of June 1, 1997.

❖ THEN *and* NOW ❖

A Barbie Doll

• • •

1959 price: $3
1959 price, adjusted for inflation: $16

1997 price: $5 to $11

PART

·3·

Business— Monkey and Otherwise

William E. Simon's List of the Greatest Economists and Business Philosophers

---

Adam Smith (1723–1790)
David Ricardo (1772–1823)
Alfred Marshall (1842–1924)
Milton Friedman (1912–)
George Stigler (1911–1991)
Joseph Schumpeter (1883–1950)
Friedrich von Hayek (1899–1992)
Ludwig von Mises (1881–1973)
James Buchanan (1919–)

Fortune's Ten Most-Admired Companies in the United States in 1996

Rank	Company
1	Coca-Cola
2	Mirage Resorts
3	Merck
4	UPS
5	Microsoft
6	Johnson & Johnson
7	Intel
8	Pfizer
9	Procter & Gamble
10	Berkshire Hathaway

Fortune's Ten Least-Admired Companies in the United States in 1996

Rank	Company
1	TWA
2	Standard Commercial
3	Kmart
4	Canandaigua Wine
5	Morrison Knudsen
6	Flagstar
7	USAir Group
8	Beverly Enterprises
9	Amerco
10	Cal Fed Bancorp

The Largest United States Businesses, by Revenues, 1995

Firm	Revenues (millions of dollars)	Assets (millions of dollars)
General Motors	168,829	217,123
Ford Motor	137,137	243,283
Exxon	110,009	91,296
Wal-Mart	93,627	37,871
AT&T	79,609	88,884
IBM	71,940	80,292
General Electric	70,028	228,035
Mobil	66,724	42,138
Chrysler	53,195	53,756
Philip Morris	53,139	53,811

❖ THEN *and* NOW ❖

A Gallon of Milk, a Loaf of Bread, a Dozen Eggs, a Pound of Butter, and a Pound of Ground Beef

• • •

1947 cost: $3.10
1947 cost, adjusted for inflation: $23

1997 cost: $8

America's Fastest-Growing Companies

Rank	Company	Annual Revenue Growth Rate (%)
1	Polyphase	233
2	America Online	215
3	Benton Oil & Gas	170
4	CNS	146
5	Oxford Health Plans	130
6	Applied Extrusion Technologies	112
7	McAfee Associates	110
8	Ha-Lo Industries	107
9	Steris	105
10	Colonial Data Technologies	100

❖ THEN *and* NOW ❖

A Bottle of Coca-Cola

• • •

1947 price: 5 cents (for 6.5 ounces)
1947 price, adjusted for inflation: 40 cents

1997 price: 90 cents (for 20 ounces)

The Ten Oldest Companies in the United States

Rank	Company	Year Founded
1	J. E. Rhoads and Sons	1702
2	Covenant Life Insurance	1717
3	Philadelphia Contributionship	1752
4	Dexter	1767
5	D. Landreth Seed	1784
6	Bank of New York	1784
7	Mutual Assurance	1784
8	Bank of Boston	1784
9	George R. Ruhl & Sons	1789
10	Burns & Russell	1789

❖ THEN *and* NOW ❖

Annual per Capita Consumption of Soft Drinks

• • •

1947: 11 gallons per person

1996: 51 gallons per person

Great States to Start a Business

The communities below offer low taxes, a highly educated citizenry, and reasonable labor expenses.

State	Star Attractions
Alabama	Booming export-based economy
Arizona	Highly educated workforce; good climate
Georgia	Low taxes; Atlanta is capital of the South
South Dakota	Leader in deregulation; low-cost and efficient workforce
Mississippi	Low taxes; both political parties are pro-business
Nebraska	Educated workforce; low taxes
Tennessee	Industrial giant of the South; skilled workforce
New Hampshire	Highly educated workforce; low taxes
Wisconsin	Aggressive pro-business government; educated and skilled workforce
Nevada	Low taxes; the high-tech mecca of the twenty-first century

Winners of the Malcolm Baldrige Quality Award

Year	Winners
1996	ADAC Laboratories
	Dana Commercial Credit Corp.
	Custom Research, Inc.
	Trident Precision Manufacturing, Inc.
1995	Armstrong World Industries
	Corning
1994	AT&T Consumer Communications Services
	GE Directories
	Wainwright Industries
1993	Eastman Chemical
	Ames Rubber
1992	AT&T Network Systems Group
	Texas Instruments
	AT&T Universal Card Services
	Ritz-Carlton Hotel
	Granite Rock
1991	Solectron
	Zytec
	Marlow Industries
1990	Cadillac Motor Car
	IBM Rochester (Minn.)
	Federal Express
	Wallace
1989	Milliken & Company
	Xerox Business Products and Systems

United States Gross Domestic Product, 1959–1996

Year	Gross Domestic Product (billions of dollars)	Year	Gross Domestic Product (billions of dollars)
1959	513.8	1978	2,411.7
1960	523.9	1979	2,650.1
1961	562.6	1980	2,911.6
1962	592.9	1981	3,183.9
1963	632.8	1982	3,295.5
1964	675.1	1983	3,665.4
1965	747.7	1984	3,994.4
1966	807.1	1985	4,285.1
1967	855.6	1986	4,501.4
1968	937.3	1987	4,836.2
1969	1,002.0	1988	5,204.9
1970	1,052.3	1989	5,537.9
1971	1,150.9	1990	5,781.5
1972	1,287.9	1991	6,002.3
1973	1,435.3	1992	6,383.0
1974	1,549.7	1993	6,688.6
1975	1,709.1	1994	7,083.2
1976	1,880.8	1995	7,350.6
1977	2,101.2	1996	7,716.1

Delinquency Rates on Bank
Installment Loans, 1980–1995

| Loan Type | *Percentage of Delinquent Loans* | | | |
	1980	*1985*	*1990*	*1995*
Personal	3.53	3.63	3.37	2.81
Auto	1.81	1.64	2.22	1.87
Home equity	N/A	2.06	1.45	1.41
Mobile home	3.14	2.39	3.03	4.02
Visa/MasterCard bank card	2.72	2.95	2.86	3.34

❖ **THEN** *and* **NOW** ❖

A Hershey's Chocolate Bar

• • •

1947 price: 5 cents (for 1 ounce)
1947 price, adjusted for inflation: 37 cents

1997 price: 55 cents (for 1.55 ounces)

Influential Business Management Books
of the Twentieth Century

Seven Habits of Highly Effective People, by Stephen R. Covey

Quality, Productivity, and Competitive Position, by W. Edwards Deming

General and Industrial Management, by Henri Fayol

My Life and Work, by Henry Ford

Motion Study, by Frank Gilbreth

Work and the Nature of Man, by Frederick Herzberg

Motivation and Personality, by Abraham Maslow

In Search of Excellence, by Thomas J. Peters

Principles of Scientific Management, by Frederick Taylor

The Largest Labor Unions
in the United States

Union	Number of Members
National Education Association	2,200,000
International Brotherhood of Teamsters	1,550,000
United Food and Commercial Workers International Union	1,375,000
American Federation of State, County and Municipal Employees	1,300,000
International Union, United Automobile, Aerospace and Agricultural Implement Workers of America	1,050,000
Service Employees International Union	950,000
American Federation of Teachers	860,000
International Brotherhood of Electrical Workers	850,000
Laborers' International Union of North America	700,000
United Steelworkers of America	650,000

❖ THEN *and* NOW ❖

Union Members as a Percentage
of the Workforce

• • •

1947: 33.7 percent

1995: 14.9 percent

Employee Benefits in the United States
for Midsize and Large Firms

	1980	1985	1989	1993
Percentage of large firms with defined benefit plans	84	80	63	56
Percentage of large firms with flexible benefits	—	—	9	12
Average days of paid holidays per year	10.1	10.1	9.2	10.2
Percentage of firms with paid holidays	99	98	97	91
Percentage of firms with paid vacations	100	99	97	97
Average vacation days after one year of employment	8.7	8.7	9.1	9.4
Average vacation days after ten years of employment	15.7	15.9	16.5	16.6
Average vacation days after 20 years of employment	20.6	20.7	20.4	20.4
Percentage of firms with medical benefits	97	96	92	82
Percentage of firms with child-care benefits	—	—	5	7

Major Strikes in America, 1980–1995

The table shows the number of work stoppages in the United States involving 1,000 workers or more.

Year	Number of Major U.S. Strikes
1981	145
1982	96
1983	81
1984	62
1985	54
1986	69
1987	46
1988	40
1989	51
1990	44
1991	40
1992	35
1993	35
1994	45
1995	31

❖ THEN *and* NOW ❖

Employee Benefits as a Percentage of Payroll

• • •

1951: 19 percent

1994: 41 percent

United States Unemployment Rate, 1961–1997

Year	Rate (%)	Year	Rate (%)
1961	6.0	1979	6.0
1962	5.5	1980	7.2
1963	5.5	1981	8.5
1964	5.0	1982	10.8
1965	4.0	1983	8.3
1966	3.8	1984	7.3
1967	3.8	1985	7.0
1968	3.4	1986	6.6
1969	3.5	1987	5.7
1970	6.1	1988	5.3
1971	6.0	1989	5.4
1972	5.2	1990	6.3
1973	4.9	1991	7.3
1974	7.2	1992	7.4
1975	8.2	1993	6.5
1976	7.8	1994	5.4
1977	6.4	1995	5.6
1978	6.0	1996	5.3
		1997*	5.0

*As of June 1, 1997.

The Top Ten Months for Merger and Acquisition Volume in American History

Rank	Month and Year	Volume (billions of dollars)
1	April 1996	102
2	August 1995	102
3	January 1997*	81
4	November 1996	75
5	October 1988	72
6	August 1996	71
7	October 1996	60
8	June 1995	56
9	March 1989	55
10	July 1995	54

*Through January 30.

❖ THEN *and* NOW ❖

McDonald's Hamburger

• • •

1955 price: 15 cents
1955 price, adjusted for inflation: 90 cents

1997 price: 59 cents

Deals of the Year: The 20 Top Mergers and Acquisitions of 1996

Rank	Companies (buyer listed first)	Value (billions of dollars)
1	British Telecommunications MCI Communications	25.36
2	Bell Atlantic Nynex	23.68
3	SBC Communications Pacific Telesis Group	16.69
4	Boeing McDonnell Douglas	14.65
5	Worldcom MFS Communications	13.48
6	Nationsbank Boatman's Bankshares	9.81
7	CSX Conrail	9.46
8	Gillette Duracell International	8.53
9	Aetna Life & Casualty U.S. Healthcare	8.22
10	Duke Power Panenergy	7.45
11	Lockheed Martin Loral	6.77
12	U.S. West Media Group Continental Cablevision	4.91

Rank	Companies (buyer listed first)	Value (billions of dollars)
13	Cisco Systems Stratacom	4.84
14	Fresenius AG National Medical Care	4.60
15	Westinghouse Electric Infinity Broadcasting	4.06
16	Staples Office Depot (deal now in the courts)	3.81
17	Thomson West Publishing	3.42
18	Munich RE American RE	3.27
19	Northrup Grumman Westinghouse Electric	3.00
20	Hughes Electronics Panamsat	3.00

❖ THEN *and* NOW ❖

A Cup of Coffee

• • •

1947 price: 5 cents (at a Woolworth's counter)
1947 price, adjusted for inflation: 37 cents

1997: $1.27 (at Starbucks)

United States Merger and Acquisition Activity Since 1983 (Announced)

Year	Total Value (millions of dollars)	Number of Mergers and Acquisitions
1983	96,185.0	3,385
1984	169,139.4	3,619
1985	186,931.7	2,257
1986	212,936.8	3,148
1987	208,718.1	3,315
1988	334,662.0	3,917
1989	292,683.0	5,455
1990	175,392.5	5,650
1991	135,550.4	5,258
1992	149,052.9	5,520
1993	235,124.2	6,315
1994	347,933.4	7,567
1995	453,268.3	9,124
1996	142,922.0	2,852

❖ THEN *and* NOW ❖

Percentage of Food Dollars
Spent on Food Away from Home

• • •

1955: 25 percent

1996: 46 percent

The 30 Largest Credit Unions
in the United States, by Total Assets

Name	State	Total Assets (December 1996)
1. U.S. Central	Kansas	$17,924,652,635
2. Western Corporate	California	9,672,375,005
3. Navy	Virginia	8,921,691,292
4. State Employees'	North Carolina	4,268,258,557
5. Southwest Corporate	Texas	2,660,466,984
6. Pentagon	Virginia	2,471,890,732
7. Boeing Employees'	Washington	2,254,646,016
8. United Airlines Employees'	Illinois	2,104,172,910
9. American Airlines Employees'	Texas	1,947,454,000
10. The Golden 1	California	1,844,548,282
11. Alaska USA	Alaska	1,709,696,313
12. Hughes Aircraft Employees	California	1,661,001,927
13. Orange County Teachers	California	1,621,261,227
14. Citizens Equity	Illinois	1,514,723,396
15. Central Corporate	Michigan	1,507,876,354
16. Suncoast Schools	Florida	1,460,659,591
17. Empire Corporate	New York	1,366,592,151
18. Mid-States Corporate	Illinois	1,364,395,809
19. Mid-Atlantic Corporate	Pennsylvania	1,304,234,414
20. Star One	California	1,302,377,008
21. Security Service	Texas	1,204,932,854
22. Southeast Corporate	Florida	1,201,132,375
23. Patelco	California	1,184,501,888
24. ESL	New York	1,174,774,312
25. America First	Utah	1,147,723,564

Name	State	Total Assets (December 1996)
26. JAX Navy	Florida	1,146,263,896
27. Wescom	California	1,072,356,117
28. Pennsylvania State Employees	Pennsylvania	1,071,669,578
29. ENT	Colorado	1,060,158,815
30. Delta Employees	Georgia	1,042,334,348

❖ THEN *and* NOW ❖

Monthly Medicare Part B Premium

• • •

1966: $3
1966, adjusted for inflation: $14

1997: $43.80

The 25 Largest FDIC-Insured Banks
in the United States, by Total Assets

Bank	Location	Total Assets (Dec. 31, 1996)
1. Chase Manhattan	New York City	$272,429,000
2. Citibank	New York City	241,006,000
3. Bank of America	San Francisco	180,480,000
4. Morgan Guaranty Trust	New York City	172,562,891
5. Wells Fargo	San Francisco	99,165,167
6. Bankers Trust	New York City	90,430,000
7. NationsBank	Charlotte, N.C.	80,870,158
8. P.N.C. Bank	Pittsburgh	57,284,961
9. Bank of New York	New York City	52,120,460
10. First National Bank of Chicago	Chicago	51,622,906
11. Home Savings FSB	Irwindale, Calif.	49,564,191
12. Republic National Bank of New York	New York City	46,952,900
13. NationsBank of the South	Atlanta	46,776,149
14. Fleet National Bank	Springfield, Mass.	46,580,793
15. First National Bank of Boston	Boston	45,874,949
16. Corestates Bank	Philadelphia	42,670,362
17. Great Western FSB	Chatsworth, Calif.	40,136,456
18. First Union National Bank of Florida	Jacksonville, Fla.	39,259,452
19. Barnett Bank	Jacksonville, Fla.	39,208,823
20. NationsBank of Texas	Dallas	39,149,395
21. First Union National Bank of North Carolina	Charlotte, N.C.	32,421,535
22. State Street Bank and Trust	Boston	31,389,728
23. Union Bank of California	San Francisco	29,197,382
24. Keybank	Cleveland	27,812,911
25. First Union National Bank	Avondale, Pa.	27,128,369

The Number of Banks in the United States

The table shows the number of FDIC-insured commercial banks and banking offices (including branches) in recent history.

Year	Banks	Total Banking Offices and Branches
1982	14,451	54,234
1983	14,469	55,322
1984	14,496	56,295
1985	14,417	57,710
1986	14,210	58,602
1987	13,723	59,080
1988	13,137	59,518
1989	12,715	60,720
1990	12,347	62,753
1991	11,927	63,896
1992	11,466	63,401
1993	10,960	63,828
1994	10,452	65,597
1995	9,943	66,455
1996	9,528	67,316

❖ THEN *and* NOW ❖

Number of U.S. Farms

• • •

1947: 5.9 million

1997: 2.1 million

Bank Closings in
the United States, 1975–1996

The table shows the number of banks (FDIC "Bank Insurance Fund" institutions) closed because of financial difficulties.

Year	Number	Year	Number
1975	13	1986	138
1976	16	1987	184
1977	6	1988	200
1978	7	1989	206
1979	10	1990	168
1980	10	1991	124
1981	10	1992	120
1982	42	1993	41
1983	48	1994	13
1984	79	1995	6
1985	120	1996	5

Total, 1934–74   514

Total 1934–96   2,080

Top Places in America to Avoid Bankers (as of December 1996)

The table shows U.S. Counties with *no* FDIC-insured commercial banks and *no* FDIC-supervised savings banks.

State	*County*
Alaska	Bristol Bay
	Denali
	Lake and Peninsula
	Wade Hampton
	Yakutat
	Yukon-Koyukuk
California	Alpine
	Sierra
Georgia	Echols
	Quitman
Hawaii	Kalawao
Idaho	Boise
Montana	Golden Valley
	Petroleum
	Yellowstone National Park
North Dakota	Slope
Nebraska	McPherson
New Mexico	Catron
Nevada	Esmeralda
South Dakota	Buffalo
	Shannon

State	County
Texas	Borden
	Hartley
	Kenedy
	King
	Loving
Utah	Daggett
Virginia	Manassas Park (city)

❖ **THEN** *and* **NOW** ❖

Number of Grocery Stores
in United States

• • •

1950: 529,000

1995: 128,000

Bank Prime Lending Rate on
Short-Term Business Loans*

Year	Rate (%)	Year	Rate (%)
1949	2.0000	1973	8.0217
1950	2.0692	1974	10.1983
1951	2.5550	1975	7.8625
1952	3.0000	1976	6.8400
1953	3.1692	1977	6.8242
1954	3.0525	1978	9.0567
1955	3.1567	1979	12.6658
1956	3.7700	1980	15.2658
1957	4.2017	1981	18.8700
1958	3.8333	1982	14.8608
1959	4.4775	1983	10.7942
1960	4.8208	1984	12.0425
1961	4.5000	1985	9.9333
1962	4.5000	1986	8.3325
1963	4.5000	1987	8.2033
1964	4.5000	1988	9.3150
1965	4.5350	1989	10.8733
1966	5.6250	1990	10.0092
1967	5.6333	1991	8.4633
1968	6.3125	1992	6.2517
1969	7.9571	1993	6.0000
1970	7.9100	1994	7.1383
1971	5.7233	1995	8.8292
1972	5.2483	1996	8.2750
		1997[†]	8.5000

*Averages of daily figures.
[†]As of June 1, 1997.

Discount Rate Changes, 1934–1996

Date	Rate (%)
February 2, 1934	1.50
August 27, 1937	1.00
October 30, 1942	0.50
April 25, 1946	1.00
January 12, 1948	1.25
August 13, 1948	1.50
August 21, 1950	1.75
January 16, 1953	2.00
February 5, 1954	1.75
April 16, 1954	1.50
April 15, 1955	1.75
August 5, 1955	2.00
September 9, 1955	2.25
November 18, 1955	2.50
April 13, 1956	2.75
August 24, 1956	3.00
August 23, 1957	3.50
November 15, 1957	3.00
January 24, 1958	2.75
March 7, 1958	2.25
April 18, 1958	1.75
September 12, 1958	2.00
November 7, 1958	2.50
March 6, 1959	3.00
May 29, 1959	3.50
September 11, 1959	4.00
June 10, 1960	3.50
August 12, 1960	3.00
July 17, 1963	3.50
November 24, 1964	4.00
December 6, 1965	4.50

Date	Rate (%)
April 7, 1967	4.00
November 20, 1967	4.50
March 22, 1968	5.00
April 19, 1968	5.50
August 30, 1968	5.25
December 18, 1968	5.50
April 4, 1969	6.00
November 13, 1970	5.75
December 4, 1970	5.50
January 8, 1971	5.25
January 22, 1971	5.00
February 19, 1971	4.75
July 16, 1971	5.00
November 19, 1971	4.75
December 17, 1971	4.50
January 15, 1973	5.00
February 26, 1973	5.50
May 4, 1973	5.75
May 11, 1973	6.00
June 11, 1973	6.50
July 2, 1973	7.00
August 14, 1973	7.50
April 25, 1974	8.00
December 9, 1974	7.75
January 10, 1975	7.25
February 5, 1975	6.75
March 10, 1975	6.25
May 16, 1975	6.00
January 16, 1976	5.50
November 22, 1976	5.25
August 30, 1977	5.75
October 26, 1977	6.00
January 9, 1978	6.50
May 11, 1978	7.00

Date	Rate (%)
July 3, 1978	7.25
August 21, 1978	7.75
September 22, 1978	8.00
October 16, 1978	8.50
November 1, 1978	9.50
July 20, 1979	10.00
August 17, 1979	10.50
September 19, 1979	11.00
October 8, 1979	12.00
February 16, 1980	13.00
May 28, 1980	12.00
June 13, 1980	11.00
July 28, 1980	10.00
September 26, 1980	11.00
November 17, 1980	12.00
December 4, 1980	13.00
May 5, 1981	14.00
November 2, 1981	13.00
December 4, 1981	12.00
July 20, 1982	11.50
August 2, 1982	11.00
August 16, 1982	10.50
August 27, 1982	10.00
October 12, 1982	9.50
November 22, 1982	9.00
December 14, 1982	8.50
April 9, 1984	9.00
November 21, 1984	8.50
December 24, 1984	8.00
May 20, 1985	7.50
March 7, 1986	7.00
April 21, 1986	6.50
July 11, 1986	6.00
August 21, 1986	5.50

Date	Rate (%)
September 4, 1987	6.00
August 9, 1988	6.50
February 24, 1989	7.00
December 19, 1990	6.50
February 1, 1991	6.00
April 30, 1991	5.50
September 13, 1991	5.00
November 6, 1991	4.50
December 20, 1991	3.50
July 2, 1992	3.00
May 17, 1994	3.50
August 16, 1994	4.00
November 15, 1994	4.75
February 1, 1995	5.25
January 31, 1996	5.00

❖ THEN *and* NOW ❖

Average Miles per Gallon

• • •

1960: 14

1994: 22

The Ten Largest Life Insurance Companies in the United States, Ranked by Total Assets

Company	State	Total Assets
1. Prudential Insurance Company of America	New Jersey	$179,734,198,510
2. Metropolitan Life Insurance Co.	New York	142,131,925,912
3. New York Life Insurance Co.	New York	59,414,522,691
4. Connecticut General Life Insurance	Connecticut	57,912,571,014
5. Northwestern Mutual Life Insurance	Wisconsin	54,873,319,994
6. Principal Mutual Life	Iowa	51,268,197,817
7. John Hancock Mutual Life	Massachusetts	50,776,577,765
8. Hartford Life Insurance Co.	Connecticut	46,640,677,616
9. Aetna Life Insurance	Connecticut	46,124,045,570
10. Lincoln National Life Insurance Co.	Indiana	43,291,889,930

❖ THEN and NOW ❖

Admission to Disneyland for an Adult/Child

• • •

1956 costs: $1/50 cents
1956 costs, adjusted for inflation: $6/$3

1996 costs: $34/$26

New Housing Starts, 1964–1997

The figures show new privately owned housing units started in structures with one unit.

Year	Housing Starts	Year	Housing Starts
1964	11,750,000	1981	8,530,000
1965	11,522,000	1982	7,956,000
1966	9,320,000	1983	12,779,000
1967	10,076,000	1984	13,181,000
1968	10,804,000	1985	12,851,000
1969	9,785,000	1986	14,189,000
1970	9,771,000	1987	13,850,000
1971	13,751,000	1988	12,994,000
1972	15,731,000	1989	12,075,000
1973	13,608,000	1990	10,807,000
1974	10,587,000	1991	10,019,000
1975	10,693,000	1992	12,381,000
1976	13,998,000	1993	13,567,000
1977	17,248,000	1994	14,293,000
1978	17,018,000	1995	12,970,000
1979	14,060,000	1996	13,829,000
1980	10,260,000	1997*	5,708,000

*As of June 1, 1997.

F.H.A. 30-Year Secondary Market
Year-End Mortgage Rates 1964–1997

Year	Rate (%)	Year	Rate (%)
1964	5.450	1981	15.980
1965	5.510	1982	12.820
1966	6.810	1983	13.230
1967	6.770	1984	12.900
1968	7.360	1985	11.280
1969	8.480	1986	9.260
1970	8.900	1987	10.760
1971	7.620	1988	10.630
1972	7.570	1989	9.690
1973	8.780	1990	9.810
1974	9.510	1991	8.690
1975	9.410	1992	8.540
1976	8.450	1993	7.510
1977	8.810	1994	9.530
1978	10.040	1995	7.510
1979	12.410	1996	8.140
1980	14.470	1997*	8.550

*As of May 1, 1997.

Top 20 United States Exporters

Firm	Exports (millions of dollars)
General Motors, Detroit, Mich.	16,127.1
Ford Motor, Dearborn, Mich.	11,892.0
Boeing, Seattle, Wash.	11,844.0
Chrysler, Highland Park, Mich.	9,400.0
General Electric, Fairfield, Conn.	8,110.0
Motorola, Schaumberg, Ill.	7,370.0
IBM, Armonk, N.Y.	6,336.0
Philip Morris, New York, N.Y.	4,942.0
Archer Daniels Midland, Decatur, Ill.	4,675.0
Hewlett-Packard, Palo Alto, Calif.	4,653.0
Intel, Santa Clara, Calif.	4,561.0
Caterpillar, Peoria, Ill.	4,510.0
McDonnell Douglas, Berkeley, Mo.	4,235.0
E. I. du Pont de Nemours, Wilmington, Del.	3,625.0
United Technologies, Hartford, Conn.	3,108.0
Eastman Kodak, Rochester, N.Y.	2,600.0
Lockheed, Calabasas, Calif.	2,079.0
Compaq Computer, Houston, Tex.	2,018.0
Raytheon, Lexington, Mass.	1,867.0
Digital Equipment, Maynard, Mass.	1,830.7

William E. Simon's
Notable Sources of Economic Wisdom

Bert Lance: "If it ain't broke, don't fix it."

Willie Sutton: When asked why he robbed banks, he answered, "Because that's where the money is."

P. T. Barnum: "There's a sucker born every minute."

H. L. Mencken: "No one ever went broke underestimating the intelligence of the American public."

Yogi Berra: "When you come to a fork in the road, take it," and "Success is ninety percent hard work, and the other half is luck."

Senator Everett Dirksen: "A billion here, a billion there, and pretty soon you're talking about real money."

Movie mogul Samuel Goldwyn: "If people don't want to come to your movies, you can't stop them."

Where's the Money?

States having the largest commercial bank deposits as of June 30, 1996.

State	Deposits (billions of dollars)	Percent of Total
New York	602.5	19.0
California	321.5	10.1
Pennsylvania	184.3	5.8
Illinois	181.4	5.7
Texas	168.2	5.3
Florida	130.5	4.1
North Carolina	121.4	3.8
Ohio	117.0	3.7
All other	1,348.2	42.5
Total U.S. bank deposits*	3,175.0	100.0

*Does not include savings banks or U.S. branches of foreign banks.

❖ **THEN** *and* **NOW** ❖

Birthrate per 1,000 Women
of Childbearing Age

• • •

1947: 113

1992: 69

PART

• 4 •

The Guys in Government

Bill Proxmire's Favorite Golden Fleece Awards

Wisconsin Senator William Proxmire issued a Golden Fleece Award every month between March 1975 and December 1988. These are his favorites.

$84,000 grant to discover why people fall in love. (National Science Foundation)

$2,500 grant to find out why people cheat when they play tennis. (National Endowment for the Humanities)

$46,000 to find out how long it takes to make breakfast. (United States Department of Agriculture)

$102,000 to find out whether sunfish that drink tequila are more aggressive than sunfish that drink gin. (National Institute on Alcohol Abuse and Alcoholism)

$27,000 to determine why prisoners want to escape from jail. (Law Enforcement Assistance Administration)

$35,000 to cover fuel expenses for a group of federal officials to give seminars on fuel conservation. (Federal Energy Administration)

$417,000 to find ways to allow meteorologists to read rain gauges without getting wet. (National Weather Service)

$4,000,000 for an advertising campaign to encourage Americans to write more letters. (United States Postal Service)

$100,000 to purchase a 100-foot steel baseball bat. (General Services Administration)

$20,000 in 1981 to construct an 800-foot limestone replica of the Great Wall of China in Bedford, Indiana. (Economic Development Administration of the Commerce Department)

$219,592 to develop a curriculum to teach college students how to watch television. (Office of Education)

$6,000 to prepare a 17-page document that told the federal government how to buy a bottle of Worcestershire Sauce. (Department of the Army)

$45 million for a study on how to cut toenails. (Health Care Financing Administration)

$1,200,000 to preserve a Trenton, N.J., sewer as a historical monument. (Environmental Protection Agency)

The Ten *Highest*-Paid Governors in the United States*

State	Salary
New Jersey	$130,000
New York	130,000
Pennsylvania	125,000
Illinois	123,022
Michigan	121,166
Washington	121,000
California	120,000
Maryland	120,000
Ohio	115,762
Minnesota	114,500

*In 1997.

The Ten *Lowest*-Paid Governors in the United States*

State	Salary
Montana	$59,310
Arkansas	60,000
Nebraska	65,000
Rhode Island	69,900
Colorado	70,000
Maine	70,000
Oklahoma	70,000
North Dakota	71,042
Arizona	75,000
Indiana	77,200

*In 1997.

1997 Salaries of
Selected Federal Employees

President of the United States	$200,000
Vice president of the United States	171,500
Speaker of the House	171,500
Chief Justice of the United States	171,500
Associate justices of the Supreme Court	164,100
President pro tempore of the Senate	148,400
Majority and minority leaders of the House and Senate	148,400
Cabinet members	148,400
Judges, U.S. courts of appeals	141,700
Judges, U.S. district courts	133,600
Deputy secretaries of State, Defense, Treasury	133,600
Deputy attorney general	133,600
Secretaries of the Army, Navy, Air Force	133,600
Senators and representatives	133,600
Undersecretaries of executive departments	123,100
Army general, 25 years of service (Grade O-10)	118,145
Army second lieutenant, two years of service (Grade O-1)	20,574
Army buck private (Grade E-1)	10,500

United States Government Employees, 1946–1997

Year	Number of Federal, State, and Local Employees
1946	5,462,000
1947	5,469,000
1948	5,765,000
1949	5,826,000
1950	6,169,000
1951	6,479,000
1952	6,704,000
1953	6,635,000
1954	6,824,000
1955	7,007,000
1956	7,454,000
1957	7,664,000
1958	7,926,000
1959	8,194,000
1960	8,419,000
1961	8,705,000
1962	9,038,000
1963	9,398,000
1964	9,785,000
1965	10,366,000
1966	11,091,000
1967	11,576,000
1968	12,026,000
1969	12,340,000
1970	12,701,000
1971	13,053,000
1972	13,542,000
1973	13,919,000
1974	14,397,000
1975	14,797,000
1976	14,947,000
1977	15,410,000
1978	15,762,000

Year	Number of Federal, State, and Local Employees
1979	16,082,000
1980	16,210,000
1981	15,895,000
1982	15,824,000
1983	15,864,000
1984	16,150,000
1985	16,552,000
1986	16,873,000
1987	17,200,000
1988	17,568,000
1989	17,952,000
1990	18,305,000
1991	18,505,000
1992	18,722,000
1993	18,962,000
1994	19,234,000
1995	19,347,000
1996	19,524,000
1997	19,582,000*

*As of April 1997.

❖ THEN and NOW ❖

Federal Budget

• • •

1947 budget: $34.5 billion (with a $4 billion *surplus*)
1947 budget, adjusted for inflation:
$254 billion (with a $29 billion *surplus*)

1995 budget: $1.5 trillion (with a $164 billion *deficit*)

Who's Minding the Store?
Key Federal Government Officials of 1997

EXECUTIVE BRANCH

President of the United States	William Clinton
Vice president of the United States	Albert Gore
Secretary of State	Madeleine Albright
Secretary of Defense	William Cohen
Secretary of the Interior	Bruce Babbitt
Secretary of Commerce	William Daley
Secretary of Housing and Urban Development	Andrew Cuomo
Secretary of Energy	Federico Peña
Secretary of Education	Richard Riley
Secretary of Veterans Affairs	Jesse Brown
Secretary of Health and Human Services	Donna Shalala
Secretary of Transportation	Rodney Slater
Secretary of Labor	Alexis Herman
Secretary of Agriculture	Dan Glickman
Secretary of the Treasury	Robert Rubin
Attorney general	Janet Reno
Chief of staff	Erskine Bowles
Domestic policy adviser	Bruce Reed
National security adviser	Sandy Berger
Chairman of the National Economic Council	Gene Sperling

LEGISLATIVE BRANCH—HOUSE

Speaker of the House	Newt Gingrich (Georgia)
Majority leader	Richard Armey (Texas)
Majority whip	Tom DeLay (Texas)
Minority leader	Richard Gephardt (Missouri)

Minority whip	David Bonior (Michigan)
Agriculture Committee chairman	Bob Smith (Oregon)
Appropriations Committee chairman	Bob Livingston (Louisiana)
Banking Committee chairman	Jim Leach (Iowa)
Budget Committee chairman	John Kasich (Ohio)
Commerce Committee chairman	Tom Bliley (Virginia)
Education and the Workplace Committee chairman	Bill Goodling (Pennsylvania)
Government and Reform Oversight Committee chairman	Dan Burton (Indiana)
House Oversight Committee chairman	Bill Thomas (California)
International Relations Committee chairman	Ben Gilman (New York)
Judiciary Committee chairman	Henry Hyde (Illinois)
National Security Committee chairman	Floyd Spence (South Carolina)
Resources Committee chairman	Don Young (Alaska)
Rules Committee chairman	Gerald Solomon (New York)
Science Committee chairman	James Sensenbrenner (Wisconsin)
Small Business Committee chairman	James Talent (Missouri)
Transportation and Infrastructure Committee chairman	Bud Shuster (Pennsylvania)
Veterans' Affairs Committee chairman	Bob Stump (Arizona)
Ways and Means Committee chairman	Bill Archer (Texas)

LEGISLATIVE BRANCH—SENATE

Majority leader	Trent Lott (Mississippi)
Majority whip	Don Nickles (Oklahoma)
Minority leader	Tom Daschle (South Dakota)
Minority whip	Wendell Ford (Kentucky)

President pro tempore	Strom Thurmond (South Carolina)
Aging Committee chairman	Charles Grassley (Iowa)
Agriculture Committee chairman	Richard Lugar (Indiana)
Appropriations Committee chairman	Ted Stevens (Alaska)
Armed Services Committee chairman	Strom Thurmond (South Carolina)
Banking Committee chairman	Alfonse D'Amato (New York)
Budget Committee chairman	Pete Domenici (New Mexico)
Commerce Committee chairman	John McCain (Arizona)
Energy and Natural Resources Committee chairman	Frank Murkowski (Alaska)
Environment and Public Works Committee chairman	John Chafee (Rhode Island)
Finance Committee chairman	Bill Roth (Delaware)
Foreign Relations Committee chairman	Jesse Helms (North Carolina)
Governmental Affairs Committee chairman	Fred Thompson (Tennessee)
Indian Affairs Committee chairman	Ben Nighthorse Campbell (Colorado)
Intelligence Committee chairman	Richard Shelby (Alabama)
Judiciary Committee chairman	Orrin Hatch (Utah)
Labor and Human Resources Committee chairman	James Jeffords (Vermont)
Rules and Administration Committee chairman	John Warner (Virginia)
Small Business Committee chairman	Christopher Bond (Missouri)
Veterans' Affairs Committee chairman	Arlen Specter (Pennsylvania)

JUDICIAL BRANCH

Chief Justice of the United States   William Rehnquist
(Arizona)

Associate justices of the Supreme Court   John Paul Stevens
(Illinois)

Sandra Day O'Connor
(Arizona)

Antonin Scalia (D.C.)

Anthony Kennedy
(California)

David Souter (New
Hampshire)

Clarence Thomas (D.C.)

Ruth Bader Ginsburg
(D.C.)

Stephen Breyer
(Massachusetts)

❖ **THEN** *and* **NOW** ❖

Salary of Mayor of Cedar Rapids, Iowa

• • •

1947 salary: $4,500
1947 salary, adjusted for inflation: $33,150

1997 salary: $62,000

William E. Simon's List
of Our Greatest Presidents

George Washington
Thomas Jefferson
Abraham Lincoln
James Madison
Theodore Roosevelt
Franklin Roosevelt
Ronald Reagan
Richard Nixon
Harry Truman
Dwight Eisenhower

❖ **THEN** *and* **NOW** ❖

Pensions for Former Presidents

• • •

1947: $0 for Herbert Hoover

1997: $148,400 each for all living former presidents

Don Rumsfeld's Rules on Politics, Congress, and the Press

First rule of politics: You can't win unless you're on the ballot.

Second rule: You can't lose unless you're running. So realize that if you're running, you may lose.

And if you tie, you do not win.

Politics is human beings. It's addition rather than subtraction.

The winner is not always the swiftest, surest, or smartest. It's the one willing to get up at five A.M. and go to train stations and plant gates to meet the workers.

In politics and government, every day is filled with numerous opportunities for serious error. So enjoy it.

The most overlooked danger for a politician is overexposure.

When someone with a rural accent says, "I don't know anything about politics," grab your wallet.

Don't necessarily avoid sharp edges. Occasionally they may be necessary to leadership.

"The oil can is mightier than the sword." (Attributed to the late Senator Everett Dirksen of Illinois)

Arguments of convenience lack integrity and inevitably trip you up.

Know and remember where you came from.

Know that Members of the U.S. House and the Senate are not there by accident. Each one managed to get there for some reason, though it may not initially be obvious. Discover it and you will learn something important about our country and its people.

Assume that with the press there's no "off the record."

Give the press one of three possible responses: (1) "I know and can tell you"; (2) "I know and can't tell you"; or (3) "I don't know." (The "Rather Rule," from Dan Rather.)

❖ **THEN** *and* NOW ❖

Percentage of Eligible Voters
Voting in the Presidential Election

• • •

1948: 51 percent

1996: 49 percent

William E. Simon's List of the Most Destructive Ideas in Public Life

---

Abortion on demand
Multiculturalism
Progressive taxation
Euthanasia
Deficit spending
The welfare state
The Great Society
No-fault divorce
Nuclear freeze
Unilateral disarmament

How Much Is That Congressman in the Window?

The top ten political action committees, by receipts, through November 25, 1996.

Political Action Committee	Receipts
1. Emily's List	$12,460,872
2. Democratic Republican Independent Voter Education Committee	9,605,690
3. American Federation of State, County, and Municipal Employees—P E O P L E, Qualified	7,052,002
4. NRA Political Victory Fund	6,650,678
5. Association of Trial Lawyers of America Political Action Committee	5,380,418
6. UAW-V-CAP (UAW Voluntary Community Action Program)	5,117,604
7. National Education Association Political Action Committee	4,896,927
8. American Medical Association Political Action Committee	4,344,254
9. Machinists' Non-Partisan Political League	3,671,387
10. Dealers Election Action Committee of the National Automobile Dealers Association (NADA)	3,657,843

Don Rumsfeld's Rules on Keeping Your Bearings in the White House

Enjoy your stint in public service. It will be among the most interesting and challenging times of your life.

Don't ever conceive of yourself as indispensable or infallible. Charles de Gaulle said that cemeteries were full of indispensable men.

Show your family, staff, and friends that you're still the same person, despite all the publicity and notoriety accompanying your position.

Choose a first-rate deputy.

Keep a sense of humor. Remember what General Joe Stillwell reportedly said: "The higher a monkey climbs, the more you see of his behind."

Realize that the amount of criticism you receive correlates somewhat to the amount of publicity you receive.

If you are not criticized, you may not be doing much.

From the inside, the White House may look as ugly as the inside of a stomach. But don't let that panic you. Things may be going better than they look from the inside.

Identify and develop a successor.

If you are lost—"Climb, conserve, and confess" (United States Navy *SNJ Flight Manual*).

Jim Miller's United States
Government Budget Super-Surplus Years

As strange as it might seem, during the history of our Republic the federal government ran a surplus almost as many years as it ran a deficit (103 v. 104). Some of these surpluses were quite large relative to total spending. The ten "super-surplus" years are as follows:

Year	Surplus (as a % of total spending)
1835	102
1807	96
1802	91
1831	87
1832	84
1811	79
1808	72
1836	65
1830	64
1929	63

William E. Simon's
Ten Greatest Government Oxymorons

Good government
Government ethics
Government efficiency
Government solutions
Government spending cuts
Tax expenditures
Tax reform
Streamlined bureaucracy
The Department of Energy
The Department of Education
(or nearly every government department)

❖ THEN *and* NOW ❖

United States Population

•   •   •

1947: 144,126,000

1997: 267,645,000

Some of the Silliest Laws in the United States

Carmel, New York: A man cannot go outside while wearing a jacket and pants that do not match.

Ottumwa, Iowa: It is unlawful for any man to wink at any woman with whom he is unacquainted.

Los Angeles, California: It is unlawful to bathe two babies in the same tub at the same time.

Zion, Illinois: It is illegal for anyone to give lighted cigars to pets.

St. Louis, Missouri: It is illegal to sit on the curb of a city street while drinking beer from a bucket.

Hartford, Connecticut: You are not allowed to cross a street while walking on your hands.

Baltimore, Maryland: It is illegal to throw bales of hay from a second-story window within the city limits.

  It is also illegal to take a lion to the movies.

Oxford, Ohio: It is illegal for a woman to strip off her clothing while standing in front of a man's picture.

Carrizozo, New Mexico: It is forbidden for a female to appear unshaven in public (includes legs and face).

Pennsylvania: It is illegal to have more than 16 women live in a house together because that constitutes a brothel ... however, up to 120 men can live together without breaking the law.

Michigan: A woman is not allowed to cut her own hair without her husband's permission.

New York: It is against the law to throw a ball at someone's head for fun.

Washington: It is illegal to paint polka dots on the American flag.

Connecticut: In order for a pickle to officially be considered a pickle, it must bounce.

Manville, New Jersey: To keep any of the incarcerated beasts from picking up bad habits, the town decreed that it is illegal to feed whiskey or offer cigarettes to animals at the local zoo.

Tennessee: It is unlawful to sell hollow logs.

Richmond, Virginia: It is illegal to flip a coin in a restaurant to see who pays for the coffee.

Pacific Grove, California: There is a $500 fine for bothering butterflies.

Hayden, Arizona: It is illegal to disturb bullfrogs within the city limits.

Spokane, Washington: It is illegal to purchase a television on Sunday.

Lehigh, Nebraska: It is illegal to sell donut holes.

North Carolina: It is illegal to use elephants to plow cotton fields.

Boston, Massachusetts: It is illegal to take more than two baths a month within Boston's confines.

Pennsylvania: In certain sections of Pennsylvania, automobiles traveling on country roads at night must send up a rocket every mile, then wait ten minutes for the road to clear.

Utah: It is against the law to fish from horseback.

Bexley, Ohio: Slot machines may not be installed or used in outhouses.

Harthahorne, Oklahoma: It is unlawful to put any hypnotized person in a display window.

Miami, Florida: It is illegal for men to wear any kind of strapless gown in public.

Nicholas County, West Virginia: No member of the clergy is allowed to tell jokes or humorous stories from the pulpit during a church service.

California: Animals are banned from mating publicly within 1,500 feet of a tavern, school, or place of worship.

Kentucky: No female weighing between 90 and 200 pounds can appear in a bathing suit on any highway within this state unless she is escorted by at least two officers or unless she is armed with a club.

Grand Haven, Michigan: There is a five-dollar fine for throwing an abandoned hoopskirt into any street or on any sidewalk.

Glendale, California: Horror films may only be shown in theaters on Mondays, Tuesdays, or Wednesdays.

Cicero, Illinois: It is illegal to hum on public streets on Sundays.

Murray Weidenbaum's Ten Silliest
Federal Regulations

1. *Applying the Endangered Species Act to the construction of the San Bernardino County Medical Center required spending $3.3 million to provide a protected habitat for eight flies.* That cost came to over $400,000 for each "Delhi Sands Flower-Loving Fly," believed to be occupying the site. And then there's the case of the Tuna Cave cockroach . . .

2. *Environmental Protection Administration regulations require Anchorage, Alaska, to add 5,000 pounds of fish waste each day to its sewage water.* That is what it takes to comply with the EPA ruling that 30 percent of the organic material in sewage be removed before the sewage reaches the ocean—Anchorage's sewage didn't have enough organic material.

3. *The National Labor Relations Board prevented a supermarket from letting the Girl Scouts use their premises because they didn't grant "equal access" to unions urging customers to boycott them.*

4. *A 1992 federal law prohibits home builders from installing toilets that hold more than 1.6 gallons of water.* This supposed conservation rule often means that it now takes two or three flushes for the equipment to do its job.

5. *The Occupational Safety and Health Administration bans gum chewing while roofing.* OSHA also requires training employees on the hazards of exposure to such deadly material as lumber and dish-washing detergent.

6. *Federal regulators ordered a Kansas City bank to put a Braille keypad on a drive-through ATM.* To be installed on the driver's side, the device apparently was designed to help blind drivers!

7. *The Justice Department sued the owners of a new motel in Wall, South Dakota, for violating the Americans With Disabilities Act, even though it was the first motel in the town to provide rooms with accommodations for the hand-*

icapped. The Feds were unhappy because people in wheelchairs registered in those rooms would have difficulty using the bathrooms in other rooms.

8. *The U.S. Department of Agriculture requires farmers to dispose of millions of pounds of otherwise good peaches and nectarines simply because they are smaller than federal standards permit.* Fruit that could be sold or given away to the needy has to be left to rot.

9. *A self-employed truck mechanic in Pennsylvania was fined $202,000 and sentenced to three years in jail for allegedly messing up a "wetland."* In reality, he hauled away 7,000 old tires and rusting car parts and placed clean fill on his property—with a federal permit. EPA argued that the property was a wetland because a stream—dry for most of the year—was partly trapped by the discarded junk and created several standing pools of water.

10. *The Food and Drug Administration ordered manufacturers of vegetable cooking oils to remove the words "no cholesterol" from their labels—even though they contained no cholesterol.* The Feds ruled the claim "misleading" because some consumers might mistakenly get the impression that "no cholesterol" means something else, such as "no fat."

Jim Miller's Top Years the United States Government Reduced the National Debt

On occasion, the federal government has *reduced* the national debt. The top ten debt-reduction years are

Year	Amount of Debt Reduction
1948	$12,401,768,000
1947	4,602,121,000
1951	4,419,716,000
1956	4,086,671,000
1957	3,249,417,000
1969	3,227,957,000
1949	2,101,587,000
1952	1,705,799,000
1950	1,395,963,000
1927	1,155,365,000

❖ THEN *and* NOW ❖

Percentage of the Population
Who Smoke

• • •

1949: 44 percent

1994: 26 percent

William E. Simon's 12 Most Dangerous and Disgusting Government Phrases

Good government. Once upon a time people spoke simply of "government." This concept was an institution, erected by consensus of the community, which protected the lives of the innocent, safeguarded people's property, and guarded the shores and frontiers against invasion. It coined hard money, delivered the mail, regulated the militia, and hung horse thieves. Everyone thought of it as good, but it was not called "good" government. When government turned into "good government" it became overgrown, incompetent, intrusive, meddlesome, menacing, fraudulent, and occasionally murderous, and it levied enormous taxes, cheapened the value of the currency, and issued huge debts to pay its bills.

Tax reform. This concept once described the repealing of the tax code's accumulated special-interest subsidies and lowering the rates. Now it has come to mean identifying some politically weaker group— or some group loathesome because of its success in creating the country's wealth and prosperity—upon whom an ever growing tax burden can be shifted. Not for nothing have most tax reform bills been labeled (by their critics, not their sponsors) "The Lawyer's and Accountant's Relief Act of 19XX."

Public-private partnership. This particularly malignant concept describes the enlisting of private sector entities to carry out grand schemes conceived by government. In return for doing what the government wants, certain "private" (and politically well-connected) business firms are handsomely rewarded. Such a partnership may be a tactical improvement over a wholly government-run scheme to effect the same ends, but it is rarely as beneficial as when the government has no scheme at all and minds its constitutional business.

Honest Congressman. There are, admittedly, some persons who fairly answer this description. But the very act of clawing one's way upward in politics to win a seat in Congress, and the need to raise $8,000 every week for two years to defend a contested seat in the next election, considerably dilute the notion of "honest." The term has now come to mean a Congressman who, once bought, stays bought. Or a Congressman who hasn't been caught lying, stealing, or bouncing checks in a respectable length of time during which the similar transgressions of others have preempted the news.

Benefit the poor. This phrase appears in reference to government programs erected in the name of the poor, blind, halt, lame, dyslexic, hungry, disadvantaged, infected, homeless, unbalanced, victimized, helpless, or lacking television of color. It is hard to spend billions without doing some (gross, if not net) good to the class for which the money is spent, but the inevitable consequence of such programs is to enrich an enormous class of individuals who minister to the needs of the poor, etc., and whose lobby groups provide the main impetus for creating and funding the program. Charitable efforts by real people, organizations, churches, etc., to actually benefit the poor do not, of course, qualify.

Fiscal conservative/social liberal. This is the modern description of a social liberal. The former unadorned version—just plain "liberal"— has been made politically dangerous by a truculent and mean-spirited electorate inflamed by right-wing talk-show hosts.

Did nothing wrong. This is the stock reply of choice for politicians accused of any sort of wrongdoing. Its great value is that it makes unnecessary any factual response to an accusation. Example: "Isn't it true you summoned your employee to a Little Rock hotel room, dropped your trousers, and sought to have your way with her?" Reply: "I did nothing wrong, and therefore there was no wrongdoing, since nothing wrong was done."

Mistakes were made. Also known as the "Reno Defense," after Attorney General Janet Reno, who in 1993 approved an order for forces under her control to destroy a compound in Waco, Texas, burning to death the 83 people whom her forces had not already shot. In the four years since, it has become a welcome addition to the rhetoric of governmental officials, since it successfully avoids giving any indication of just who made the mistakes.

❖ **THEN** *and* NOW ❖

The Top Tax Rate

• • •

1947: 86.5 percent

1997: 39.6 percent

Don Rumsfeld's
Rules on Serving in Government

Government employees are there to serve the American people. Do it well.

It is tough to spend "federal [the taxpayers'] dollars" so that the intended result is achieved. This truth is not well understood.

Beware when any idea is pushed primarily because it is "bold, exciting, innovative, and new." Loads of "bold, exciting, innovative, and new ideas" are also foolish.

Think of the federal government as the last resort, not the first. As former Missouri congressman Tom Curtis said, "Public money drives out private money."

Strive to make proposed solutions as self-executing as possible. As the degree of discretion increases, so too does bureaucracy, delay, and expense.

Include others. As New York's Senator Pat Moynihan once said, "Stubborn opposition to proposals often has no other basis than the complaining question, 'Why wasn't I consulted?' "

Watch for the "Not invented here" syndrome.

Another Moynihanism worth remembering: "The atmosphere in which social legislation is considered is not a friend of truth."

If in doubt, don't.

If still in doubt, do what's right.

Treat each federal dollar you handle as if you had earned it.

"The objective of dedicated employees should be to analyze situations intelligently, anticipate problems prior to their occurrence, have answers to those problems, and move swiftly to solve them. However, when you're up to your ears in alligators, it is difficult to remember that the reason you're here is to drain the swamp" (author unknown).

"In Washington, D.C., the size of a farewell party is often directly proportional to the departing person's new position and their prospective ability to dispense largess" (Devon G. Cross).

"Every government looking at the actions of another government and trying to explain them always exaggerates rationality and conspiracy, and underestimates incompetency and fortuity" (Silberman's Law of Diplomacy, United States Circuit Court Judge Laurence Silberman).

❖ THEN *and* NOW ❖

Compton's Encyclopedia

• • •

1947 cost for a full set: $95
1947 cost, adjusted for inflation: $700

1997 cost for the software version: $50

A World of Business

Maceo K. Sloan's Top Ten
African Stock Markets

Rank	Market	Market Capitalization (millions of dollars)
1.	Johannesburg Stock Exchange	241,571
2.	Cairo Stock Exchange	14,173
3.	Casablanca Stock Exchange	8,705
4.	Tunisia Stock Exchange	4,263
5.	Zimbabwe Stock Exchange	3,635
6.	Nigerian Stock Exchange	3,560
7.	Nairobi Stock Exchange	1,846
8.	Stock Exchange of Mauritius	1,676
9.	Ghana Stock Exchange	1,493
10.	Abidjian Stock Exchange	914

The World's Major Equity Markets' Returns in 1996

Country (Index)	Nominal Return	Dollar Return
Australia (All Ordinaries)	10.00	2.25
Canada (Toronto Exchange 300-Stock Index)	26.00	26.70
France (CAC-40)	24.00	17.20
Germany (DAX Index)	28.00	18.80
India (Sensex)	−1.40	−3.90
Italy (BCI Index)	13.00	17.80
Japan (Nikkei 225)	−3.70	−13.90
Mexico (IPC)	21.00	18.10
Singapore (Straits Times Industrials)	−2.20	−1.20
South Korea (Korea Composite)	−1.30	−9.60
Spain (Madrid General Index)	39.00	30.40
Switzerland (Swiss Market Index)	20.00	5.10
Taiwan (Weighted-Price Index)	34.00	33.00
United Kingdom (Financial Times 100)	12.00	4.30
United States (Dow-Jones Industrial Average)	26.00	26.00

International Currency Exchange Rates— Units per U.S. Dollar

Country	Monetary Unit	1997	1996	1995	1994
Australia*	Dollar	0.7550	0.7828	0.7407	0.7316
Austria	Schilling	12.270	10.589	10.076	11.409
Belgium	Franc	35.970	30.968	29.472	33.426
Canada	Dollar	1.3810	1.3638	1.3725	1.3664
China (People's Republic)	Yuan	8.3207	8.3395	8.3700	8.6404
Denmark	Krone	6.6379	5.8009	5.5999	6.3561
European Community*	ECU	1.1266	1.2520	1.2941	1.1862
Finland	Markka	5.1941	4.5948	4.3763	5.2340
France	Franc	5.8752	5.1158	4.9864	5.5459
Germany	Deutsch mark	1.7438	1.5049	1.4321	1.6216
Greece	Drachma	274.59	240.82	231.68	242.50
Hong Kong	Dollar	7.7475	7.7345	7.7357	7.7290
India	Rupee	35.850	35.510	32.418	31.394
Ireland*	Pound	1.5130	1.5995	1.6035	1.4969
Italy	Lira	1,699.30	1,542.76	1,629.45	1,611.49
Japan	Yen	114.61	108.78	93.96	102.18
Malaysia	Ringgit	2.5245	2.5154	2.5073	2.6237
Mexico	Peso	7.9520	7.6004	6.4467	3.3853
Netherlands	Guilder	1.9630	1.6863	1.6044	1.8190
New Zealand*	Dollar	0.6790	0.6877	0.6563	0.5936
Norway	Krone	7.3283	6.4594	6.3355	7.0553
Portugal	Escudo	175.98	154.28	149.88	165.93
Singapore	Dollar	1.43	1.4100	1.4171	1.5275
South Africa	Rand	4.5385	4.3042	3.6284	3.5526
South Korea	Won	890.00	805.00	772.69	806.93
Spain	Peseta	147.300	126.68	124.64	133.88

*Value is in U.S. dollars.

Country	Monetary Unit	1997	1996	1995	1994
Sri Lanka	Rupee	58.540	55.289	51.047	49.170
Sweden	Krona	7.7345	6.7082	7.1406	7.7161
Switzerland	Franc	1.4606	1.2361	1.1812	1.3667
Taiwan	Dollar	27.820	27.468	26.495	26.465
Thailand	Baht	25.150	25.359	24.921	25.161
United Kingdom*	Pound	1.6650	1.5607	1.5785	1.5319
United States[†]	Dollar	95.77	87.34	84.25	91.32

*Value is in U.S. dollars.
[†]U.S. dollar value is the index of the weighted average exchange value of the U.S. dollar against currencies of other G-10 countries (March 1973 = 100).

❖ THEN *and* NOW ❖

Per Capita Consumption
of Red Meat/Poultry

• • •

1947: 113 pounds/15 pounds

1996: 111 pounds/66 pounds

The Average Annual Inflation Rate for Selected Countries, 1990–1995

Country	Inflation Rate (%)
Australia	2.51
Austria	3.24
Canada	2.24
Chile	13.83
Denmark	1.98
Egypt	12.31
Finland	2.29
France	2.22
Greece	13.94
Hong Kong	9.26
Indonesia	8.98
Italy	5.01
Japan	1.36
Jordan	4.26
South Korea	6.20
Mexico	66.30
Netherlands	2.73
Norway	2.38
Philippines	10.39
Russian Federation*	563.87
Singapore	2.57
South Africa	11.26
Spain	5.16
Sri Lanka	10.28
Sweden	4.18
Turkey	79.67
United Kingdom	3.40
United States	3.12
Uruguay	60.93

*Four-year average using 1991 as the base year.

Growth Rates in EU Member States' Economies, by Gross Domestic Product

Country	1995 Real Growth in GDP (%)
Ireland	10.7
Finland	4.2
Sweden	3.6
Norway	3.3
Luxembourg	3.2
Italy	3.0
Denmark	2.8
Spain	2.8
United Kingdom	2.5
Portugal	2.5
France	2.2
Netherlands	2.1
Iceland	2.1
Greece	2.0
Belgium	1.9
Germany	1.9
Austria	1.4
Switzerland	0.1

Global Interest Rates, 1996

Country	Short-Term Rates (%)	Long-Term Rates (%)
Mexico	33.0	34.0
Italy	9.5	9.0
New Zealand	9.3	7.9
Spain	7.6	8.9
Australia	7.2	8.2
Sweden	5.9	8.1
United Kingdom	5.9	7.8
Ireland	5.5	7.5
United States	5.0	6.5
Norway	4.8	6.6
Canada	4.4	7.6
Denmark	4.0	7.2
France	3.9	6.6
Finland	3.7	6.0
Germany	3.3	6.3
Belgium	3.2	6.4
Austria	3.1	5.4
Netherlands	3.0	6.3
Switzerland	1.9	4.0
Japan	0.6	3.2

Gross Domestic Product of Nations

Country	Gross Domestic Product (billions of dollars)
Afghanistan	12.80
Albania	4.10
Algeria	108.70
Andorra	1.00
Angola	7.40
Antigua and Barbuda	0.43
Argentina	279.00
Armenia	9.10
Australia	405.40
Austria	152.00
Azerbaijan	11.50
Bahamas	4.80
Bahrain	7.30
Bangladesh	144.50
Barbados	2.50
Belarus	49.20
Belgium	197.00
Belize	0.58
Benin	7.60
Bhutan	1.30
Bolivia	20.00
Bosnia and Herzegovina	1.00
Botswana	4.50
Brazil	977.00
Brunei	4.60
Bulgaria	43.20
Burkina Faso	7.40
Burundi	4.00
Cambodia	7.00
Cameroon	16.50

Country	Gross Domestic Product (billions of dollars)
Canada	694.00
Cape Verde	0.44
Central African Republic	2.50
Chad	3.30
Chile	113.20
China (People's Republic)	3,500.00
Colombia	192.50
Comoros	0.37
Congo	16.50
Congo (Republic of)	7.70
Costa Rica	18.40
Croatia	20.10
Cuba	14.70
Cyprus	7.80
Czech Republic	106.20
Denmark	112.80
Djibouti	0.20
Dominica	0.20
Dominican Republic	26.80
Ecuador	44.60
Egypt	171.00
El Salvador	11.40
Equatorial Guinea	0.33
Eritrea	2.00
Estonia	12.30
Ethiopia	24.20
Fiji	4.70
Finland	92.40
France	1,173.00
Gabon	6.00
Gambia	1.10
Georgia	6.20
Germany	1,452.00

Country	Gross Domestic Product (billions of dollars)
Ghana	25.10
Greece	101.70
Grenada	0.28
Guatemala	36.70
Guinea	6.50
Guinea-Bissau	1.00
Guyana	1.60
Haiti	6.50
Honduras	10.80
Hungary	72.50
Iceland	5.00
India	1,409.00
Indonesia	711.00
Iran	324.00
Iraq	41.10
Ireland	54.60
Israel	80.10
Italy	1,088.60
Ivory Coast	21.90
Jamaica	8.20
Japan	2,679.20
Jordan	19.30
Kazakhstan	46.90
Kenya	36.80
Kiribati	0.07
Kuwait	30.80
Kyrgyzstan	5.40
Laos	5.20
Latvia	14.70
Lebanon	18.30
Lesotho	2.80
Liberia	2.30
Libya	32.90

Country	Gross Domestic Product (billions of dollars)
Liechtenstein	0.63
Lithuania	13.30
Luxembourg	10.00
Macedonia	1.90
Madagascar	11.40
Malawi	6.90
Malaysia	193.60
Maldives	0.39
Mali	5.40
Malta	4.40
Marshall Islands	0.09
Mauritania	2.80
Mauritius	10.90
Mexico	721.40
Micronesia	0.21
Moldova	10.40
Monaco	0.79
Mongolia	4.90
Morocco	87.40
Mozambique	12.20
Myanmar (Burma)	47.00
Namibia	5.80
Nauru	0.10
Nepal	25.20
Netherlands	301.90
New Zealand	62.30
Nicaragua	7.10
Niger	5.50
Nigeria	135.90
North Korea	21.50
Norway	106.20
Oman	19.10
Pakistan	274.20

Country	Gross Domestic Product (billions of dollars)
Palau	0.82
Panama	13.60
Papua New Guinea	10.20
Paraguay	17.00
Peru	87.00
Philippines	179.70
Poland	226.70
Portugal	116.20
Qatar	10.70
Romania	105.70
Russia	796.00
Rwanda	3.80
St. Kitts and Nevis	0.22
St. Lucia	0.64
St. Vincent and the Grenadines	0.24
San Marino	0.38
Sao Tome and Principe	0.14
Saudi Arabia	189.30
Senegal	14.50
Seychelles	0.43
Sierra Leone	4.40
Singapore	66.10
Slovakia	39.00
Slovenia	22.60
Solomon Islands	1.00
Somalia	3.60
South Africa	215.00
South Korea	590.70
Spain	565.00
Sri Lanka	65.60
Sudan	25.00
Suriname	1.30
Swaziland	3.60

Country	Gross Domestic Product (billions of dollars)
Sweden	177.30
Switzerland	158.50
Syria	91.20
Taiwan	290.50
Tajikistan	6.40
Tanzania	23.10
Thailand	416.70
Togo	4.10
Tonga	0.23
Trinidad and Tobago	16.20
Tunisia	37.10
Turkey	345.70
Turkmenistan	11.50
Uganda	16.80
Ukraine	174.60
United Arab Emirates	70.10
United Kingdom	1,138.40
United States	7,250.00
Uruguay	24.40
Uzbekistan	54.70
Venezuela	195.50
Vietnam	97.00
Western Samoa	0.42
Yemen	37.10
Zambia	8.90
Zimbabwe	18.40

The Relationship Between Economic Growth and Government Spending in Selected Countries

Country	Government Expenditures (as % of GNP)	Long-Term Growth in GNP, 1984–94 (%)
Sweden	67.3	1.0
Denmark	61.1	1.9
Finland	58.9	1.2
Belgium	54.6	2.0
Greece	51.2	1.6
France	51.0	2.0
Italy	50.9	2.1
Austria	47.8	2.6
Canada	46.5	2.5
Germany	45.6	2.4
Luxembourg	45.0	3.4
Spain	43.7	2.9
United Kingdom	42.7	2.4
Ireland	41.7	4.1
Australia	36.9	3.0
United States	35.8	2.6
Portugal	34.7	3.1
Japan	26.9	3.3

The Top Export Partners of the United States

Country	Country's Percentage of Total 1995 U.S. Exports
Canada	24.3
Japan	12.4
Mexico	8.8
United Kingdom	5.6
South Korea	4.9
Germany	4.3
Taiwan	3.7
Netherlands	3.2
Singapore	3.0
France	2.7
Hong Kong	2.7
Belgium	2.4
China	2.3
Brazil	2.2
Australia	2.1
Italy	1.7
Malaysia	1.7
Thailand	1.2
Switzerland	1.2
Saudi Arabia	1.2

Transactions in U.S. Stocks and Bonds by Foreign Investors in 1995

Residence of Investor	Value of U.S. Stocks Traded (billions of dollars)	Value of U.S. Corporate Bonds Traded (billions of dollars)	Total (billions of dollars)
United Kingdom	245	146	391
Canada	96	13	109
Bermuda	78	13	91
Netherlands Antilles	79	10	89
British West Indies	69	11	80
Japan	45	13	58

❖ THEN and NOW ❖

First-Class Postage Letter

• • •

1947 cost: 3 cents
1947 cost, adjusted for inflation: 22 cents

1997 cost: 32 cents

The Impact of Global Trade on State Economies

State (or D.C.)	Export Revenues (millions of dollars)	Employment from Exporting
Alabama	2,459	18,273
Alaska	485	3,717
Arizona	1,879	13,480
Arkansas	1,106	8,263
California	21,969	160,071
Colorado	1,883	13,641
Connecticut	2,189	16,937
Delaware	781	5,930
District of Columbia	491	3,516
Florida	9,372	68,021
Georgia	3,767	27,361
Hawaii	748	5,248
Idaho	588	4,381
Illinois	6,792	49,184
Indiana	3,913	28,827
Iowa	1,528	11,364
Kansas	1,383	10,441
Kentucky	2,066	15,348
Louisiana	4,136	31,212
Maine	978	7,623
Maryland	2,812	20,318
Massachusetts	4,448	32,674
Michigan	6,800	51,509
Minnesota	3,212	24,053
Mississippi	1,124	8,306
Missouri	2,591	19,378
Montana	358	2,792
Nebraska	626	4,581
Nevada	615	4,216

State (or D.C.)	Export Revenues (millions of dollars)	Employment from Exporting
New Hampshire	772	6,122
New Jersey	7,711	59,166
New Mexico	802	5,907
New York	12,979	95,553
North Carolina	3,819	28,157
North Dakota	231	1,701
Ohio	7,540	56,080
Oklahoma	1,484	10,980
Oregon	1,855	13,510
Pennsylvania	8,422	63,558
Rhode Island	550	4,113
South Carolina	2,388	17,683
South Dakota	311	2,271
Tennessee	3,084	22,672
Texas	13,125	98,711
Utah	1,071	7,982
Vermont	384	3,042
Virginia	3,886	28,241
Washington	3,905	29,604
West Virginia	1,346	10,270
Wisconsin	3,440	25,165
Wyoming	233	1,684

International Tourism Industry Receipts and Gross Domestic Product

Country	Contribution of Foreign Tourists to Country's GDP (% of GDP)
Austria	6.6
Portugal	4.7
Spain	4.5
Greece	4.1
Ireland	3.5
Switzerland	3.2
Turkey	3.2
New Zealand	3.0
Italy	2.3
Belgium	2.2
Denmark	2.2
Iceland	2.2
France	1.9
Australia	1.8
Norway	1.8
United Kingdom	1.5
Finland	1.4
Netherlands	1.4
Canada	1.4
Sweden	1.4
United States	0.9
Germany	0.5
Japan	0.1

Life Expectancy in Selected Countries, 1996

Country	Life Expectancy at Birth (years)	Country	Life Expectancy at Birth (years)
Afghanistan	45.9	Iran	67.4
Algeria	68.3	Iraq	67.0
Argentina	71.7	Israel	78.0
Australia	79.4	Italy	78.1
Austria	76.5	Japan	79.6
Belgium	77.1	Kenya	55.6
Bolivia	59.8	Mexico	73.7
Brazil	61.6	Morocco	69.5
Canada	79.1	Netherlands	77.7
China	69.6	Peru	69.1
Congo	46.7	Philippines	65.9
Cuba	75.1	Poland	72.1
Czech Republic	73.8	Russia	63.2
Denmark	77.3	Saudi Arabia	69.0
Egypt	61.4	Slovakia	73.0
Ethiopia	46.9	South Africa	59.5
Finland	75.5	South Korea	73.3
France	78.4	Spain	78.3
Georgia	68.1	Sweden	78.1
Germany	76.0	Switzerland	77.6
Greece	78.1	Syria	67.1
Haiti	49.3	Taiwan	76.0
Honduras	68.4	Thailand	68.6
Hong Kong	82.2	Turkey	71.9
Hungary	69.0	Ukraine	66.8
India	59.7	United Kingdom	76.4
Indonesia	61.6	United States	76.0

Proportion of Gross Domestic Product
Spent on Health Care
in Selected Countries, 1994

Country	Percent of GDP Spent on Health Care
Australia	8.5
Austria	9.7
Belgium	8.2
Canada	9.8
Czech Republic	7.6
Denmark	6.6
France	9.7
Germany	8.6
Greece	3.6
Iceland	8.1
Italy	8.6
Japan	7.3
Netherlands	8.8
Spain	7.3
Sweden	7.7
Switzerland	9.6
Turkey	2.6
United Kingdom	6.9
United States	14.2

The Best Countries in the World to Open a Liquor Store

Country	Proportion of Consumption Expenditures Allocated to Alcohol (%)
Australia	4.2
Canada	2.7
Denmark	3.4
France	2.0
India	0.5
Ireland	11.5
Israel	0.7
Italy	1.0
Netherlands	1.5
Norway	3.1
Russia	3.9
Singapore	2.0
South Africa	5.1
Sweden	2.9
United Kingdom	6.2
United States	1.1

❖ THEN *and* NOW ❖

A Fifth of Jim Beam in Dodge City, Kansas

• • •

1947 price: $5
1947 price, adjusted for inflation: $37

1997 price: $11

U.S. Federal Debt Held by Foreign Investors

Year	Seasonally Adjusted End-of-Month Totals (billions of dollars)	Year	Seasonally Adjusted End-of-Month Totals (billions of dollars)
1961	13.2	1979	118.0
1962	15.1	1980	128.5
1963	15.6	1981	135.4
1964	16.4	1982	148.3
1965	16.3	1983	165.4
1966	14.1	1984	205.4
1967	15.3	1985	225.2
1968	13.9	1986	264.2
1969	10.9	1987	300.5
1970	20.3	1988	362.2
1971	46.7	1989	428.2
1972	55.5	1990	455.6
1973	56.0	1991	488.4
1974	58.8	1992	546.1
1975	66.8	1993	619.2
1976	78.0	1994	684.5
1977	109.1	1995	856.6
1978	132.1	1996	1,124.1

The Top Ten U.S. Trading Partners in 1996

Country	1996 Total Trade (billions of dollars)
Canada	290.17
Japan	182.76
Mexico	129.72
China	63.47
Germany	62.42
United Kingdom	59.81
South Korea	49.25
Taiwan	48.32
Singapore	37.03
France	33.06

The Top Ten Countries with Which the United States Had a Trade Deficit in 1996

Country	Jan.–Nov. 30, 1996 Deficit (millions of dollars)
Japan	−47,683
China	−39,517
Canada	−22,838
Mexico	−16,202
Germany	−15,469
Taiwan	−11,498
Italy	−9,437
Malaysia	−9,304
Venezuela	−8,162
Thailand	−5,033

The Top Ten Countries with Which the United States Had a Trade Surplus in 1996

Country	Jan.–Nov. 30, 1996 Surplus (millions of dollars)
Netherlands	9,997
Australia	8,137
Brazil	5,779
Belgium	4,088
South Korea	3,938
Hong Kong	3,916
Argentina	2,481
Egypt	2,237
Chile	2,031
United Arab Emirates	2,024

The Largest Merchant Fleets in the World, 1996

Country	Number of Ships
Panama	3,626
Liberia	1,581
Russia	1,553
Cyprus	1,456
China	1,448
Malta	998
Greece	963
Bahamas	935
Japan	775
Norway	648
Singapore	637
St. Vincent and the Grenadines	606
Philippines	520
United States	512
Turkey	445

❖ THEN and NOW ❖

Average Federal Income Tax

• • •

1947: $328
1947, adjusted for inflation: $2,420

1994: $4,585

Employee and Employer Share of
Social Security Taxes for Selected Countries, 1995

Old age, disability, and survivor's insurance.

Country	Employee's Social Security Tax Rate (% of income)	Employer's Social Security Tax Rate (% of wage)
Netherlands	22.65	0.00
Austria	10.25	12.55
United Kingdom	10.00	10.20
Germany	9.30	9.30
France	9.05	8.20
Italy	8.34	21.30
Japan	8.25	8.25
Norway	7.80	14.20
Ireland	7.75	12.20
Belgium	7.50	8.86
United States	6.20	6.20
Switzerland	4.90	4.90
Spain	4.70	23.60
Canada	2.70	2.70
Sweden	1.00	18.83

Individual Income Taxes
Around the World

Country	Lowest Tax Rate on Personal Income (%)	Highest Tax Rate on Personal Income (%)
Netherlands	13.0	60.0
France	5.0	56.8
Spain	20.0	56.0
Belgium	25.0	55.0
Germany	19.0	53.0
Italy	10.0	51.0
Japan	10.0	50.0
Turkey	25.0	50.0
Luxembourg	10.0	50.0
Austria	10.0	50.0
Ireland	27.0	48.0
Australia	20.0	47.0
Denmark	22.0	40.0
Portugal	15.0	40.0
Greece	5.0	40.0
United Kingdom	20.0	40.0
United States*	15.0	39.6
Finland	7.0	39.0
Mexico	3.0	35.0
Iceland	34.3	34.3
New Zealand	24.0	33.0
Canada	17.0	29.0
Sweden	20.0	20.0
Norway	9.5	13.7
Switzerland	1.0	13.2

*When you add in other provisions of the tax code, plus possible state, regional, and local taxes, the United States moves to near the top of the list.

Corporate Income Taxes Around the World

Country	Percent of Total Tax Receipts Paid by Corporations	Country	Percent of Total Tax Receipts Paid by Corporations
Luxembourg	16.3	Canada	5.7
Japan	14.9	Spain	5.7
Australia	12.8	Greece	5.0
New Zealand	10.6	Turkey	4.9
Italy	9.3	Belgium	4.8
Ireland	8.1	Sweden	4.5
Norway	8.1	Denmark	4.4
United States	7.9	Germany	3.6
Portugal	7.2	Austria	3.5
United Kingdom	7.2	France	3.4
Netherlands	7.0	Iceland	3.0
Switzerland	5.8	Finland	2.7

❖ THEN *and* NOW ❖

Flight from Kansas City, Mo., to Paris,
with a Connection in New York City

• • •

1947 fare: $674 (flight time: 37 hours)
1947 fare, adjusted for inflation: $4,290

1997 fare: $740 (flight time: 10 hours, 30 minutes)

Road Kill: Highway Death Rates
Around the World

Country	Annual Highway Deaths per 100,000 Population
Portugal	29
Greece	21
Luxembourg	18
Austria	17
Belgium	17
Czech Republic	16
France	16
New Zealand	16
United States	16
Spain	14
Turkey	14
Italy	12
Germany	12
Australia	11
Canada	11
Denmark	11
Ireland	11
Japan	10
Switzerland	10
Finland	9
Netherlands	8
Norway	7
Sweden	7
United Kingdom	7
Iceland	6

PART

So Many
Interesting
People

Don Rumsfeld's Rules of Life (and Other Things)

"You can't pray a lie."—*Huckleberry Finn* by Mark Twain

"It takes everyone to make a happy day."—Marcy Rumsfeld at age seven

"Persuasion is a two-edged sword, reason and emotion; plunge it deep."—Attributed to the late professor Lewis Sarett, Sr.

"The art of listening is indispensable for the right use of the mind. It is also the most gracious, the most open, and most generous of human habits."—Unknown

"In writing, if it takes over thirty minutes to write the first two paragraphs, select another subject."—The late Raymond Aron

"In unanimity there may well be either cowardice or uncritical thinking."—Unknown

"If you're coasting, you're going downhill."—The late L. W. Pierson, Sr.

"First law of holes: If you get in one, stop digging."—Arnold Langbo, CEO, Kellogg Company

"Behold the turtle. He makes progress only when he sticks his neck out."—Attributed to James Bryant Conant

"The harder I work, the luckier I am."—Unknown

"If it doesn't go easy, force it."—George D. Rumsfeld's assessment of his son Don's operating principle at age ten

"But I am me."—Nick Rumsfeld at age nine

Perspective: Maurice Chevalier's reported response when asked how it felt to reach 80—"Pretty good, considering the alternative."

"For every human problem there is a solution that is simple, neat and wrong."—The late H. L. Mencken

"Simply because a problem is shown to exist, it doesn't necessarily follow that there is a solution."—Unknown

"If a problem has no solution, it is not a problem, but a fact, not to be solved, but to be coped with over time."—Shimon Peres, former Prime Minister of Israel

"If you develop rules, never have more than ten."—Don Rumsfeld

❖ **THEN** *and* NOW ❖

A Pack of Camel Cigarettes

• • •

1947 price: 20 cents
1947 price, adjusted for inflation: $1.50

1997 price: $2.90

The Healthiest Places*
to Live in the United States

Rank	Location
1	Rochester, Minnesota
2	Iowa City, Iowa
2 (tie)	Charlottesville, Virginia
4	Columbia, Missouri
5	La Crosse, Wisconsin
6	San Francisco, California
7	Roanoke, Virginia
8	Sioux Falls, South Dakota
9	Asheville, North Carolina
10	Greenville, North Carolina
11	Madison, Wisconsin
12	Tyler, Texas
13	Portland, Maine
14	Reno, Nevada
15	Santa Rosa, California
16	Bismarck, North Dakota
17	Lexington, Kentucky
18	Seattle, Washington
19	Spokane, Washington
20	Springfield, Missouri

*With populations of at least 100,000.

Bob Nagy's List
of Notable U.S. Hospitals

State (or D.C.)	Name of Hospital
Alabama	University of Alabama Hospital, Birmingham
Arizona	University Medical Center of the University of Arizona, Health Sciences Center, Tucson
California	UCLA Medical Center, Los Angeles
Colorado	Craig Hospital, Englewood
	University Hospital of the University of Colorado Health Sciences Center, Denver
Connecticut	Yale–New Haven Hospital, New Haven
District of Columbia	Georgetown University Medical Center
Florida	Jackson Memorial Medical Center, Miami
Georgia	Emery University Hospital, Atlanta
Illinois	University of Chicago Hospitals, Chicago
Indiana	Indiana University Medical Center, Indianapolis
Iowa	University of Iowa Hospitals and Clinics, Iowa City
Kansas	Menninger Memorial Hospital, Topeka
Louisiana	Ochsner Clinic and Hospital, New Orleans
Maryland	Johns Hopkins Medical Institutions, Baltimore
Massachusetts	Massachusetts General Hospital, Boston
Michigan	University of Michigan Medical Center, Ann Arbor
Minnesota	Mayo Clinic and Hospitals, Rochester
Missouri	Barnes Hospital, St. Louis

State (or D.C.)	Name of Hospital
Nebraska	University Hospital at the University of Nebraska Medical Center, Omaha
New Hampshire	Dartmouth Hitchcock Medical Center, Hanover
New Jersey	St. Barnabas Medical Center, Livingston
New York	Memorial Sloan-Kettering Cancer Center, New York
North Carolina	Duke University Medical Center, Durham
Ohio	Cleveland Clinic, Cleveland
Oregon	Oregon Health Sciences University Hospital, Portland
Pennsylvania	Hospital of the University of Pennsylvania, Philadelphia
	Presbyterian University Hospital, Pittsburgh
Tennessee	Vanderbilt University Hospital, Nashville
Texas	University of Texas M.D. Anderson Cancer Center, Houston
Utah	University of Utah Hospital and Clinics, Salt Lake City
Virginia	Medical College of Virginia Hospitals, Richmond
	University of Virginia Hospital, Charlottesville
Washington	University of Washington Medical Center, Seattle
Wisconsin	University of Wisconsin Hospital and Clinics, Madison

William E. Simon's
Timeless Oxymorons

Honest lawyers
Objective reporters
Balanced newspaper articles or newscasts

❖ THEN *and* NOW ❖

Salary of Member
of the United States Congress

• • •

1947 annual salary: $12,500
1947 annual salary, adjusted for inflation: $92,090

1997 annual salary: $133,600

The 50 Busiest Airports
in the United States

Ranked by 1995 enplanements.

Airport	City	Enplanements
Chicago O'Hare International	Chicago	31,433,002
The William B. Hartsfield Atlanta Airport	Atlanta	28,090,978
Dallas–Fort Worth International	Dallas–Fort Worth	26,962,940
Los Angeles International	Los Angeles	26,133,795
San Francisco International	San Francisco	17,187,766
Miami International	Miami	16,065,673
Denver International	Denver	14,858,763
JFK International	New York	14,601,827
Detroit Metropolitan Wayne County	Detroit	14,082,598
Phoenix Sky Harbor International	Phoenix	13,738,433
McCarran International	Las Vegas	13,243,748
Newark International	Newark	13,230,961
Lambert–St. Louis International	St. Louis	12,790,701
Minneapolis–St. Paul International	Minneapolis–St. Paul	12,559,491
General Edward Lawrence Logan Airport	Boston	11,734,693
Houston Intercontinental	Houston	11,350,898
Honolulu International	Honolulu	11,283,295
Seattle-Tacoma International	Seattle	11,077,470
Orlando International	Orlando	10,583,166
Charlotte-Douglas International	Charlotte	10,463,122
La Guardia	New York	10,297,628

Airport	City	Enplanements
Pittsburgh International	Pittsburgh	9,945,793
Philadelphia International	Philadelphia	8,791,372
Salt Lake City International	Salt Lake City	8,741,761
Cincinnati–Northern Kentucky	Covington-Cincinnati	7,504,549
Washington National	Arlington	7,373,178
San Diego International-Lindbergh	San Diego	6,636,372
Baltimore-Washington International	Baltimore	6,466,755
Washington Dulles International	Loudon, Va.	5,879,523
Tampa International	Tampa	5,567,950
Portland International	Portland	5,537,790
Cleveland-Hopkins International	Cleveland	5,270,004
Metropolitan Oakland International	Oakland	4,797,498
Fort Lauderdale–Hollywood	Fort Lauderdale	4,787,467
Kansas City International	Kansas City	4,743,009
Luis Muñoz Marin International	San Juan, P.R.	4,609,099
San Jose International	San Jose	4,394,931
Memphis International	Memphis	4,323,207
Chicago Midway	Chicago	4,266,831
New Orleans International	New Orleans	4,084,886
William P. Hobby	Houston	3,905,727
Nashville International	Nashville	3,685,219
John Wayne Airport–Orange County	Santa Ana	3,533,073
Dallas Love Field	Dallas	3,418,604
Sacramento Metropolitan	Sacramento	3,346,762
Ontario International	Ontario	3,232,996
Indianapolis International	Indianapolis	3,189,932
Albuquerque International	Albuquerque	3,056,442
San Antonio International	San Antonio	3,028,246
Raleigh-Durham International	Raleigh-Durham	2,938,831

Winners of the Nobel Prize
in Economic Sciences, 1969–1996

Year	Winner(s)	Contribution
1969	Ragnar Frisch (Norway) and Jan Tinbergen (Netherlands)	Advances in applied dynamic economic processes models
1970	Paul A. Samuelson (United States)	Developments in static and dynamic economic theory
1971	Simon Kuznets (United States)	Economic growth theory
1972	Kenneth J. Arrow (United States) and Sir John R. Hicks (United Kingdom)	Contributions to general economic equilibrium theory and welfare theory
1973	Wassily Leontief (United States)	Development of the input-output method
1974	Gunnar Myrdal (Sweden) and Friedrich August von Hayek (Austria)	Work in the theory of money and economic fluctuations
1975	Leonid Vitaliyevich Kantorovich (USSR) and Tjalling C. Koopmans (Netherlands-United States)	Theory of optimum allocation of resources
1976	Milton Friedman (United States)	Consumption analysis, monetary history and theory
1977	Bertil Ohlin (Sweden) and James E. Meade (United Kingdom)	Contribution to the theory of international trade and international capital movements

Year	Winner(s)	Contribution
1978	Herbert A. Simon (United States)	Decision-making process within economic organizations
1979	Sir Arthur Lewis (United Kingdom) and Theodore W. Schultz (United States)	Economic development research
1980	Lawrence R. Klein (United States)	Advances in econometrics
1981	James Tobin (United States)	Analysis of financial markets
1982	George J. Stigler (United States)	Industrial structures, functioning of markets and causes and public regulation
1983	Gerard Debreu (France-United States)	Reformulation of the theory of general equilibrium
1984	Sir Richard Stone (United Kingdom)	Development of systems of national accounts
1985	Franco Modigliani (Italy-United States)	Analyses of saving and of financial markets
1986	James M. Buchanan, Jr. (United States)	Theory of economic and political decision making
1987	Robert M. Solow (United States)	Contributions to the theory of economic growth
1988	Maurice Allais (France)	Contributions to the theory of markets and efficient utilization of resources

Year	Winner(s)	Contribution
1989	Trygve Haavelmo (Norway)	Contributions to probability theory and econometrics
1990	Merton M. Miller (United States), William F. Sharpe (United States), and Harry M. Markowitz (United States)	Contributions to financial economics (risk)
1991	Ronald H. Coase (United States–United Kingdom)	Advances in theories of transaction costs and property rights
1992	Gary S. Becker (United States)	Microeconomic behavioral analysis
1993	Robert W. Fogel (United States) and Douglass C. North (United States)	Quantitative economic history
1994	John F. Nash (United States), John C. Harsanyi (United States), and Reinhard Selten (Germany)	Equilibria in the theory of noncooperative games
1995	Robert E. Lucas, Jr. (United States)	Applications of rational expectations theory
1996	William Vickrey (United States–Canada) and James A. Mirrlees (United Kingdom)	Contributions to the economic theory of incentives under asymmetric information

Bob Nagy's List of the
Best U.S. Medical Schools, by Region

FAR WEST

University of California at San Francisco
University of Southern California
Stanford University
University of Washington

ROCKY MOUNTAINS/SOUTHWEST

University of Arizona
University of Colorado
University of Nevada, Reno
University of New Mexico
University of Oklahoma
University of Texas at Austin

SOUTH

University of Alabama, Birmingham
University of Florida
University of Louisville
University of Tennessee
Vanderbilt University

MIDWEST

University of Chicago
Northwestern University
Indiana University
University of Iowa
University of Kansas
University of Michigan
Ohio State University

ATLANTIC COAST
Georgetown University
Howard University
Johns Hopkins University
University of North Carolina at Chapel Hill

NORTHEAST
Albert Einstein College (Yeshiva University)
Columbia University
Harvard University
New York University
University of Pennsylvania
Temple University
Yale University

❖ THEN *and* NOW ❖

Family Doctor's Annual Income

• • •

1951: $13,440
1951, adjusted for inflation: $85,150

1994: $182,400

Cities with Populations of Over 200,000, Ranked by Educational Attainment

City	Percent of Elementary and High School Enrollment in Public Schools, 1990	Rank	Percent of Adults* with a B.A. Degree or Higher, 1990	Rank
New York City	79.1	67	23.0	34
Los Angeles	86.8	46	23.0	34
Chicago	79.5	66	19.5	49
Houston	92.3	17	25.1	27
Philadelphia	70.8	77	15.2	67
San Diego	91.9	18	29.8	10
Dallas	90.2	32	27.1	18
Phoenix	92.8	14	19.9	48
Detroit	87.3	44	9.6	75
San Antonio	92.5	15	17.8	57
San Jose	90.9	25	25.3	26
Indianapolis	87.2	45	21.7	40
San Francisco	77.5	71	35.0	3
Baltimore	85.5	52	15.5	65
Jacksonville	87.5	43	17.9	56
Columbus	88.4	40	24.6	28
Milwaukee	80.6	63	14.8	70
Memphis	89.3	34	17.5	59
Washington, D.C.	83.9	57	33.3	5
Boston	77.2	73	30.0	8
El Paso	94.6	5	16.2	62
Seattle	78.6	69	37.9	2
Cleveland	78.7	68	8.1	77

*Persons 25 years old and older.

City	Percent of Elementary and High School Enrollment in Public Schools, 1990	Rank	Percent of Adults* with a B.A. Degree or Higher, 1990	Rank
Nashville-Davidson, TN	84.7	55	23.6	30
Austin	93.4	10	34.4	4
New Orleans	79.7	65	22.4	37
Denver	85.9	50	29.0	11
Fort Worth	90.9	25	21.5	42
Oklahoma City	90.3	28	21.6	41
Portland, Oreg.	89.1	38	25.9	23
Long Beach, Calif.	91.6	20	23.2	32
Kansas City, Mo.	85.6	51	22.0	39
Virginia Beach, Va.	93.1	12	25.5	25
Charlotte, N.C.	89.3	34	28.4	12
Tucson	91.9	18	20.7	46
Albuquerque	91.3	23	28.4	12
Atlanta	90.3	28	26.6	20
St. Louis, Mo.	77.4	72	15.3	66
Sacramento	90.3	28	23.5	31
Fresno, Calif.	95.9	2	19.1	51
Tulsa	87.8	42	25.8	24
Oakland	86.7	48	27.2	17
Honolulu	76.1	74	27.7	15
Miami	90.3	28	12.8	73
Pittsburgh	75.8	75	20.1	47
Cincinnati	81.3	60	22.2	38
Minneapolis	84.8	54	30.3	7
Omaha	81.7	59	23.1	33
Toledo	78.5	70	14.1	71
Buffalo	84.0	56	16.0	64
Wichita	86.8	46	22.7	36

*Persons 25 years old and older.

City	Percent of Elementary and High School Enrollment in Public Schools, 1990	Rank	Percent of Adults* with a B.A. Degree or Higher, 1990	Rank
Mesa, Ariz.	96.1	1	21.0	45
Colorado Springs	93.6	9	27.5	16
Las Vegas	93.0	13	13.4	72
Santa Ana, Calif.	94.6	5	10.6	74
Tampa	88.4	40	18.7	54
Arlington, Tex.	92.5	15	30.0	8
Anaheim, Calif.	91.6	20	18.8	53
Louisville, Ky.	82.7	58	17.2	60
St. Paul	80.7	62	26.5	21
Newark	86.3	49	8.5	76
Corpus Christi	94.0	7	17.8	57
Birmingham	90.5	27	16.2	62
Norfolk, Va.	91.0	24	16.8	61
Anchorage	95.0	4	26.9	19
Aurora, Colo.	95.2	3	26.3	22
Riverside, Calif.	91.4	22	19.3	50
St. Petersburg	89.2	36	18.6	55
Rochester, N.Y.	85.5	52	19.0	52
Lexington-Fayette, Ky.	90.0	33	30.6	6
Jersey City	72.7	76	21.4	43
Baton Rouge	79.9	64	28.3	14
Akron	88.9	39	14.9	69
Raleigh-Durham	93.2	11	40.6	1
Stockton, Calif.	94.0	7	15.0	68
Richmond	89.2	36	24.2	29
Mobile	81.1	61	21.4	43

*Persons 25 years old and older.

William E. Simon's List
of God's Greatest Gifts to Mankind

Jesus Christ
Heaven
Earth
Life
The United States of America
Freedom
Liberty
Love
The Bible
Forgiveness
Faith

❖ **THEN** *and* **NOW** ❖

A Box of Eight Crayola Crayons

• • •

1947 price: 15 cents
1947 price, adjusted for inflation: $1.10

1997 price: 80 cents

Average Jury Awards to Plaintiffs in United States Civil Trials (Tort Cases)

Case Type	Average Award	Percentage of Cases Won by Plaintiff
All tort cases	$ 408,000	48
Automobile	220,000	58
Medical malpractice	1,484,000	29
Product liability	727,000	39
Professional malpractice	1,057,000	49
Slander or libel	229,000	41
Toxic substances	526,000	70

❖ THEN *and* NOW ❖

Ratio of Workers to
One Social Security Beneficiary

• • •

1947: 16.5:1

1996: 3.1:1

Bob Nagy's List of
the Best U.S. Law Schools, by Region

FAR WEST

University of California-Berkeley
University of California-Los Angeles
University of Hawaii
University of Southern California
Stanford University

ROCKY MOUNTAINS/SOUTHWEST

University of Arizona
Baylor University
University of New Mexico
Southern Methodist University
University of Texas at Austin

SOUTH

University of Alabama
University of Arkansas
University of Georgia
University of Kentucky
University of Tennessee
Vanderbilt University

MIDWEST

Case Western Reserve University
University of Chicago
University of Illinois
Indiana University
University of Kansas
University of Michigan
Northwestern University
University of Notre Dame
Ohio State University

ATLANTIC COAST

American University
Duke University
Georgetown University
Washington and Lee University
University of Virginia

NORTHEAST

Boston College
Columbia University
Cornell University
Harvard University
New York University
University of Pennsylvania
St. John's University
Yale University

William E. Simon's Notable Myths

All the news that's fit to print.
I'm from the government and I'm here to help you.
Social Security will always be there.
The check is in the mail.
We only owe it to ourselves.
We're running out of resources.
God is dead.

❖ **THEN** *and* NOW ❖

Salary of the President of the United States

• • •

1947 salary: $75,000
1947 salary, adjusted for inflation: $552,570

1997 salary: $200,000

Bob Nagy's List of the Best U.S. Accounting Schools, by Region

FAR WEST

University of Alaska, Anchorage
University of Southern California
San Diego State University
University of Oregon
University of Washington

ROCKY MOUNTAINS/SOUTHWEST

University of Colorado at Denver
University of Northern Colorado
Boise State University
Brigham Young University
Arizona State University
University of Nevada–Las Vegas
University of New Mexico
New Mexico State University
University of Oklahoma
Baylor University
University of Texas at Austin

SOUTH

University of Kentucky
Louisiana Tech University
University of Missouri–Columbia
University of Alabama
University of Florida
Florida State University
University of Georgia
Georgia State University
Mississippi State University
University of Tennessee at Knoxville

MIDWEST

University of Chicago
University of Illinois
Ball State University
University of Iowa
Kansas State University
Michigan State University
University of Nebraska–Lincoln
University of Akron
Ohio University
University of Wisconsin–Madison

ATLANTIC COAST

University of Delaware
Howard University
Towson State University
North Carolina A&T
University of North Carolina–Charlotte
Clemson University
College of William and Mary
James Madison University

NORTHEAST

University of Connecticut
Bentley College
Baruch College
New York University
Lehigh University
Pennsylvania State University

Cost per Victory in
Major League Baseball, 1996 Season

Team	Payroll (millions of dollars)	Wins	Cost per Victory (dollars)
Montreal Expos	15.4	88	175,000
Kansas City Royals	18.5	75	246,667
Oakland Athletics	19.4	78	248,718
Milwaukee Brewers	20.2	80	252,500
Minnesota Twins	22.0	78	282,051
Pittsburgh Pirates	21.3	73	291,781
San Diego Padres*	27.2	91	298,901
Houston Astros	26.9	82	328,049
New York Mets	23.5	71	330,986
Florida Marlins	30.1	80	376,250
California Angels	26.9	70	384,286
Los Angeles Dodgers*	34.6	90	384,444
Toronto Blue Jays	28.5	74	385,135

*Made playoffs.

❖ **THEN** *and* NOW ❖

Teacher's Annual Salary

• • •

1947: $2,640
1947, adjusted for inflation: $19,450

1996 annual salary: $37,850

Team	Payroll (millions of dollars)	Wins	Cost per Victory (dollars)
Texas Rangers*	35.9	90	398,889
Detroit Tigers	21.9	53	413,208
Chicago Cubs	31.5	76	414,474
St. Louis Cardinals*	38.9	88	442,045
Philadelphia Phillies	29.7	67	443,284
Seattle Mariners	38.3	85	450,588
Colorado Rockies	38.2	83	460,241
Boston Red Sox	39.4	85	463,529
Cleveland Indians*	46.2	99	466,667
Chicago White Sox	41.9	85	492,941
Atlanta Braves*	47.9	96	498,958
Cincinnati Reds	40.7	81	502,469
San Francisco Giants	34.8	68	511,765
Baltimore Orioles*	49.3	88	560,227
New York Yankees*	52.9	92	575,000

*Made playoffs.

❖ THEN *and* NOW ❖

Mail Carrier's Starting Pay

• • •

1947: $2,100
1947, adjusted for inflation: $15,470

1997: $26,060

Cost per Victory of Leading
Major League Pitchers, 1996 Season

Player	Salary (millions of dollars)	Victories	Cost per Victory (dollars)
Andy Pettitte	0.15	21	7,143
Ismael Valdez	0.43	15	28,667
Hideo Nomo	0.60	16	37,500
Kevin Ritz	0.65	17	38,235
Roger Pavlik	1.10	15	73,333
Pat Hentgen	2.25	20	112,500
Denny Neagle	2.30	16	143,750
Ken Hill	3.00	16	187,500
Kevin Brown	3.30	17	194,118
Charles Nagy	3.34	17	196,470
Mike Mussina	4.00	19	210,526
Andy Benes	4.00	18	222,222
John Smoltz	5.50	24	229,167
Alex Fernandez	4.50	16	281,250
Ramon Martinez	4.80	15	320,000

❖ THEN *and* NOW ❖

Prize for Winning the Masters Tournament

• • •

1947: $2,500
1947, adjusted for inflation: $18,420

1996: $450,000 (plus green jacket)

Cost per Victory in the NBA, 1996–1997 Regular Season

Team	Payroll	Wins	Cost per Victory
Miami*	$23,800,000	61	$ 390,000
Utah*	25,270,000	64	395,000
Charlotte*	22,430,000	54	415,000
New York*	25,930,000	57	455,000
Atlanta*	25,810,000	56	461,000
Houston*	26,250,000	57	461,000
Cleveland	20,370,000	42	485,000
Detroit*	27,210,000	54	504,000
Portland*	24,900,000	49	508,000
L.A. Lakers*	28,830,000	56	515,000
Seattle*	30,300,000	57	532,000
Minnesota*	24,350,000	40	609,000
Toronto	18,630,000	30	621,000
L.A. Clippers*	26,040,000	36	723,000
Milwaukee	24,220,000	33	734,000
Washington*	34,560,000	44	785,000
Chicago*	58,270,000	69	844,000
Sacramento	29,080,000	34	855,000
Phoenix*	36,140,000	40	904,000
New Jersey	25,430,000	26	978,000
Orlando*	45,050,000	45	1,001,000

*Made playoffs.

Team	Payroll	Wins	Cost per Victory
Golden State	$30,870,000	30	$1,030,000
Indiana	40,930,000	39	1,050,000
Dallas	26,110,000	24	1,088,000
Philadelphia	24,770,000	22	1,126,000
Denver	24,570,000	21	1,170,000
Vancouver	18,640,000	14	1,331,000
San Antonio	33,180,000	20	1,660,000
Boston	25,070,000	15	1,671,000

❖ THEN *and* NOW ❖

Mayor of San Francisco's Salary

• • •

1947 salary: $20,000
1947 salary, adjusted for inflation: $147,350

1997 salary: $141,750

Cost per Point of Leading NBA Scorers, 1996–1997 Regular Season

Player	Salary (millions of dollars)	Points Scored	Cost per Point (dollars)
Damon Stoudamire	1.5	1,634	918
Allen Iverson	2.3	1,787	1,287
Jerry Stackhouse	2.3	1,679	1,370
Scottie Pippen	2.3	1,656	1,389
Tim Hardaway	2.5	1,644	1,521
Patrick Ewing	3.0	1,751	1,713
Mitch Raymond	3.6	2,095	1,718
Glen Rice	4.0	2,115	1,891
Karl Malone	4.7	2,249	2,090
Kendall Gill	3.8	1,789	2,124
Vin Baker	3.8	1,637	2,321
Glenn Robinson	4.6	1,689	2,724
Laphonso Ellis	3.3	1,203	2,743
Grant Hill	5.0	1,710	2,924
Tom Gugliotta	5.0	1,672	2,990
Steve Smith	4.5	1,445	3,114
Latrell Sprewell	7.0	1,938	3,612
Kevin Johnson	7.0	1,410	4,965
Hakeem Olajuwon	9.7	1,810	5,359
Chris Webber	8.0	1,445	5,536
Penny Hardaway	6.7	1,210	5,537
Gary Payton	10.2	1,785	5,714
Reggie Miller	11.3	1,751	6,453
Shaquille O'Neal	10.7	1,336	8,009
Michael Jordan	30.1	2,431	12,382

Sports Salary Trivia

Major League Baseball players who made more than $1,000,000 in 1997: 280

NBA players who made more than $1,000,000 during the 1996–1997 season: 250

NHL players who made more than $1,000,000 during the 1996–1997 season: 186

NFL players who made more than $1,000,000 during the 1996 season: 343

Average annual growth in Major League Baseball salaries from 1970 to 1995: 15.5%

Average U.S. inflation rate between 1970 and 1995: 5.6%

Minimum salary of an NFL player in 1996: $131,000

Minimum salary of a Major League Baseball player in 1996: $109,000

Minimum salary of an NBA player in 1996: $220,000

Minimum salary of an NHL player in 1996: $125,000

Potential annual winnings of a thoroughbred horse: $3–$5,000,000

Potential annual winnings of a jockey: $15–$20,000,000

Fortune's Most Generous People in the United States, 1996

Name	Amount Donated (millions of dollars)
George Soros	350
L. S. Skaggs	155
Bill Gates	135
Walter Annenberg	128
William Hewlett	100
Leslie Gonda	73
Jay A. and Robert A. Pritzker	70
Ted Arison	60
Robert Galvin	60
William Davidson	35
Joan Kroc	33
Robert Bass	30
Michael Bloomberg	30
John Kluge	30
Thomas Lee	30
Ted Turner	28
Alfred Lerner	27
Jon Huntsman	25
Phil Knight	25
Fred Rose	25
James Michener	24
Peter Nicholas	23
Ross Perot	23
Joseph Jamail	20
Betty Brown Casey	18

The 20 Highest Paid
Female Executives

Name	Title and Firm	Salary	Total Compensation
Linda Wachner	CEO and President, Warnaco Group	$2,470,000	$10,190,000
	CEO and Chair, Authentic Fitness	$975,000	$975,000
	Combined:	$3,445,000	$11,165,000
Jill Barad	CEO, Mattel	$786,546	$6,170,000
Carol Bartz	Chair, CEO, and President, Autodesk	$475,000	$5,510,000
Sally Crawford	COO, Healthsource	$324,233	$4,020,000
Estée Lauder	Former Chair, Estée Lauder	$2,970,000	$3,820,000
Ngaire Cuneo	Executive VP, Conseco	$250,000	$3,680,000
Jane Hirsh	President, International Business, Copley Pharmaceutical	$380,000	$3,390,000
Nancy Pedot	CEO and President, Symboree	$370,184	$3,190,000
Donna Karan	Chair, CEO, and Chief Designer, Donna Karan International	$2,730,000	$2,730,000

Name	Title and Firm	Salary	Total Compensation
Sharon Mates	President, North American Vaccine	$273,000	$2,330,000
Amy Lipton	Senior VP and General Counsel, CUC International	$210,000	$2,230,000
Ellen Gordon	President and COO, Tootsie Roll Corporation	$665,000	$1,660,000
Charlotte Beers	Chair, Ogilvy & Mather Worldwide	$1,000,000	$1,600,000
Jane Thompson	President, Home Services, Sears, Roebuck	$375,000	$1,550,000
Lois Juliber	President, Colgate-North America, Colgate Palmolive	$370,499	$1,470,000
Dorrit Bern	Vice Chair, CEO, and President, Charming Shoppes	$438,462 (for 5½ months' employment)	$1,440,000
Mary Anne Carpenter	Executive VP, Service Products, HealthCare Compare	$215,417	$1,430,000
Christie Hefner	Chair and CEO, Playboy Enterprises	$467,316	$1,400,000
Rosemarie Greco	President and CEO, CoreStates Bank	$387,308	$1,360,000
Carol St. Mark	President, Pitney Bowes Business Services	$413,333	$1,330,000

Pete Colhoun's 11 Favorite General Sayings

1. Success is a journey, not a destination.

2. Attitude is a little thing that makes a big difference.

3. Real leaders are ordinary people with extra ordinary determination.

4. Confidence is the cocky feeling you have just before you know better.

5. Life is a grindstone. Whether it grinds you down or polishes you up depends on the stuff of which you are made.

6. When you are scared, the trick is not to rid your stomach of butterflies, but to make them fly in formation.

7. Do you want the man in charge or the woman who really knows what's going on here?

8. The world is made to be wooed by adventurous people.

9. If you don't have a competitive advantage, don't compete.

10. Happiness is not having what you want, but wanting what you have.

11. When you are young, society conditions you to exchange time for money, and this is fine. But as you become more affluent, it's somehow very difficult to reverse the process and trade money for time.

Sources and
Acknowledgments

⊖ ⊖ ⊖

Those Mad, Mad Markets

P. 5 Arthur Levitt; p. 6 derived from various newspapers, including *The Wall Street Journal, USA Today,* and *The New York Times;* p. 7 Pete Colhoun; pp. 8–9 derived from various newspapers, including *The Wall Street Journal, USA Today,* and *The New York Times;* p. 10 Mary Farrell; p. 11 derived from various newspapers, including *The Wall Street Journal, USA Today,* and *The New York Times;* p. 12 Mike Holland; p. 13 Bob Stovall; pp. 14–18 *Standard and Poor's 500 Guide;* pp. 19–22 *Standard and Poor's Security Price Index Record* and *Standard and Poor's Current Statistics;* pp. 23–26 Beth Dater; pp. 27–30 Securities Data Company and Website; pp. 31–32 Pete Colhoun; p. 33 The New York Stock Exchange; p. 34 Frank Cappiello; pp. 35–43 *Louis Rukeyser's Mutual Funds;* pp. 44–45 *The Wall Street Journal,* Morningstar Inc., and IBC; p. 46 Morningstar Inc.; pp. 47–50 *Fortune;* p. 51 *The World Almanac* and *The Wall Street Journal;* p. 52 Professor Robert Nagy, University of Wisconsin–Green Bay; pp. 53–55 Bernadette Murphy; pp. 56–57 The Federal Reserve Board; pp. 58–59 Julius Westheimer; p. 60 Frank Cappiello; p. 61 *The Statistical Abstract of the United States;* p. 62 Elaine Garzarelli; pp. 63–64 The St. Louis Federal Reserve Bank; pp. 65–66 Bob Stovall; p. 67 United States Securities and Exchange Commission, *The Statistical Abstract of the United States,* and The New York Stock Exchange; pp. 68–70 Charles R. Schwab; pp. 71–72 Pete Colhoun.

It's Your Money

Pp. 75–76 Mary Farrell; p. 77 *Kiplinger's Personal Finance Magazine;* pp. 78–79 Jim Jones; pp. 80–81 derived from the Commerce Clearing House and *Information Please Almanac;* p. 82 The Tax Foundation; p. 83 *Kiplinger's Personal Finance Magazine;* p. 84 The Internal Revenue Service; p. 85 FDIC Website; p. 86 *FDIC Annual Report;* pp. 87–88 *Kiplinger's Personal Finance Magazine;* p. 89 Pete Colhoun; pp. 90–92 United States Bureau of the Census; p. 93 Professor Robert Nagy; p. 94 *Federal*

Reserve Bulletin; p. 95 *Fortune;* p. 96 Professor Robert Nagy; pp. 97–98 United States Bureau of the Census and *The Statistical Abstract of the United States;* pp. 99–100 *Federal Reserve Bulletin;* pp. 101–103 Knight Kiplinger; p. 104 Professor Robert Nagy; p. 105 Federal Reserve Board; pp. 106–107 United States Department of Education; pp. 108–111 Kiplinger Online; pp. 112–113 United States Bureau of Labor Statistics and *The Statistical Abstract of the United States;* p. 114 St. Louis Federal Reserve Bank.

Business—Monkey and Otherwise
P. 117 William E. Simon; pp. 118–119 *Fortune;* p. 120 *The Fortune 500;* pp. 121–122 *Fortune;* p. 123 Professor Robert Nagy; p. 124 United States Department of Commerce; p. 125 St. Louis Federal Reserve (FRED Database); p. 126 *ABA Consumer Credit Delinquency Bulletin* and *The Statistical Abstract of the United States;* p. 127 Professor Robert Nagy; p. 128 *Encyclopedia of Associations* and *The Information Please Business Almanac;* p. 129 *The Statistical Abstract of the United States;* pp. 130–131 United States Department of Labor; p. 132 Securities Data Company and Website; pp. 133–134 *Fortune;* p. 135 Securities Data Company and *The Information Please Business Almanac;* pp. 136–137 NCUA Call Report Database; p. 138 Federal Deposit Insurance Corporation Institution List; p. 139 FDIC Website; p. 140 *FDIC Annual Report;* pp. 141–142 FDIC Website; pp. 143–147 Federal Reserve Board; p. 148 California State Insurance Commissioner's Office; pp. 149–150 St. Louis Federal Reserve Bank; p. 151 *Fortune;* p. 152 William E. Simon; p. 153 FDIC Website.

The Guys in Government
Pp. 157–158 Bill Proxmire; pp. 159–160 derived from *The Information Please Almanac* and *The World Almanac and Book of Facts;* pp. 161–162 *The Statistical Abstract of the United States;* pp. 163–166 *The Wall Street Journal, The New York Times,* and other newspapers; p. 167 William E. Simon; pp. 168–169 Don Rumsfeld; p. 170 William E. Simon; p. 171 The Federal Election Commission Web Page; p. 172 Don Rumsfeld; p. 173 Jim Miller; p. 174 William E. Simon; pp. 175–177 various Internet sources, including the bit.listserv.giggles newsgroup; pp. 178–179 Murray Weidenbaum; p. 180 Jim Miller; pp. 181–183 William E. Simon; pp. 184–185 Don Rumsfeld.

A World of Business
P. 189 Maceo K. Sloan; p. 190 *The Wall Street Journal, The New York Times,* and various sources on the Internet; pp. 191–192 The Federal Reserve Board; p. 193 *The Information Please Almanac* and the International Monetary Fund's International Financial Statistics; p. 194 *European Community, Eurostat News Release;* p. 195 OECD, from their Website; pp. 199–201 The CIA World Fact Book Online; p. 202 OECD in Figures; p. 203 United States Agency for International Development and the United States Department of Commerce; p. 204 United States Department of the Treasury, quarterly Treasury *Bulletin;* pp. 205–206 *Business America,* United States Department of Commerce; p. 207 OECD in Figures; p. 208 United States Bureau of

the Census and *The Statistical Abstract of The United States;* p. 209 OECD in Figures and *The Statistical Abstract of the United States;* p. 210 *The Statistical Abstract of the United States;* p. 211 the St. Louis Federal Reserve Bank; pp. 212–213 United States Bureau of the Census; p. 214 Maritime Administration, United States Department of Commerce; p. 215 United States Social Security Administration, Office of Research and Statistics, *Social Security Throughout the World*; pp. 216–218 OECD in Figures.

So Many Interesting People

Pp. 221–222 Don Rumsfeld; p. 223 *Kiplinger's Personal Finance Magazine;* pp. 224–225 Professor Robert Nagy; p. 226 William E. Simon; pp. 227–228 Federal Aviation Administration DOT/TSC CY1955 SVSIS Database; pp. 229–231 University of Chicago Web Page, *The Information Please Almanac,* and *The World Almanac;* pp. 232–233 Professor Robert Nagy; pp. 234–236 United States Department of the Census; p. 237 William E. Simon; p. 238 *United States Bureau of Justice Statistics' Civil Jury Cases and Verdicts in Large Counties*; pp. 239–240 Professor Robert Nagy; p. 241 William E. Simon; pp. 242–250 Professor Robert Nagy; p. 251 *Fortune;* pp. 252–253 *Working Woman;* p. 254 Pete Colhoun.